BY DAVID VENABLE

In the Kitchen with David:
QVC's Resident Foodie Presents
Comfort Foods That Take You Home

———

In the Kitchen with David:
QVC's Resident Foodie Presents
Back Around the Table

———

In the Kitchen with David:
QVC's Resident Foodie Presents
Comfort Food Shortcuts

QVC's Resident Foodie Presents

Comfort Food Shortcuts

David Venable

Foreword by Valerie Bertinelli

BALLANTINE BOOKS | NEW YORK

*For busy home cooks everywhere who need
time-saving shortcuts in the kitchen*

Contents

Foreword

Valerie Bertinelli

WHEN I LEARNED THAT I WOULD BE ON *IN THE KITCHEN WITH DAVID* WITH MY first cookbook, *Valerie's Home Cooking,* I couldn't believe it. David has long been my mom's favorite QVC host. Not only has she been sending me Christmas gifts from QVC for thirty years, but I've been watching *In the Kitchen with David* for as long as I can remember. To be asked to appear on David's show was a dream come true. Boy, was I happy dancing all through my house!

David and I have much in common. We both celebrate food as the most delicious part of life. Both of us also learned how to cook from our parents. David learned to cook Southern classics like smothered pork chops, buttermilk biscuits, and coconut layer cake from his mother and grandmothers, while my mother, *nonne* (grandmothers), and *zie* (aunts) taught me Italian classics like Bolognese and risotto as well as Italian-American favorites such as Italian wedding soup and spaghetti and meatballs. (In truth, I've been cooking longer than I've been acting, and I started acting when I was twelve years old.)

What you don't realize until you meet and work with David and his QVC team is how genuinely kind they are. They all support one another, and it shows. The funny, smart, generous David that you see on-screen is just as funny, smart, and generous when he's not in front of the camera. David cares so much about food and works so hard to make comfort food easy to prepare. I think David is absolutely magical.

It was such a pleasure when David took me under his culinary wing. He's been a mentor to me and helped me share my cookbooks, my recipes, and my wines on his show. During our time together we realized that we are true culinary kindred spirits. When it comes to food we think alike, as we discovered when we found that we both have recipes for tomato soup with grilled cheese sandwich croutons in our cookbooks! Inspired by the BLT sandwich, David offers a BETA (bacon, egg, tomato, and avocado) breakfast bowl in *Comfort Food Shortcuts,* while I have a BLT Pasta in *Valerie's Home Cooking.*

David is genuine. So is his food. He won't recommend anything he doesn't believe in. Like me, he wants recipes that are quick and easy, because like you, we're busy people. When we have time to prepare a long-simmering meat sauce, that's great. But more often than not these days, we're short on time. That's when David's supermarket shortcuts come to the rescue, like an all-in-one skillet breakfast with quick-cooking grits on the bottom and eggs cooked in tomato sauce. Or Chicken Potpie that takes advantage of a rotisserie chicken, condensed cream of chicken soup, and refrigerated buttermilk biscuits. And a ready-in-minutes Cookies and Cream Dip that's a spin on the old-fashioned icebox cake with chocolate wafers and prepared whipped topping.

Once you pick up David's *Comfort Food Shortcuts,* your cooking will become easier and faster. And you won't want to put down his book. Unless it's time to sit down at the table.

Introduction

WHEN YOU AND I FIRST STARTED COOKING TOGETHER SOME TWENTY-FIVE YEARS ago, ingredients that are now pantry and refrigerator basics, like hummus and pesto, were just finding their way into our kitchens. Pressure cookers, blenders, and slow cookers had yet to evolve into the multipurpose, powerful, and time-saving appliances they are today. Who would have thought that you would be able to bake a Chocolate Pudding Cake in a slow cooker? Or cook boneless country-style pork ribs in a pressure cooker in less than fifty minutes? Or air-fry Honey-Bourbon Chicken Wings in a countertop machine without oil?

Together, we're still discovering and sharing new foods and flavors. *Comfort Food Shortcuts* is my new collection of classic and contemporary recipes that are tastier, simpler, and more comforting than ever. Some recipes are creative versions of old favorites, like Philly cheesesteak ingredients turned into a hot dip, while others are regional American dishes such as Shrimp Creole, or popular international dishes like Chicken Tikka Masala.

As you know, I'm always on the lookout for an even more perfect mac 'n' cheese, new ways to make the divine swine even more divine, and oh-so-good desserts that are oh-so-much richer, creamier, and more satisfying. Whenever I run across a terrific tip, like using orzo in place of rice for an easy no-stir risotto, or a time-saving way to bake a super-moist cake using a cake mix, three eggs, and a container of your favorite melted ice cream, I can't wait to share them with you.

We are all busier than ever, and time seems to fly by, but we still want to feed our families and friends satisfying, comforting food. We still want to spend time around the dinner table together. We can do that because there are now so many ways to make cooking easier and faster.

The recipes in *Comfort Food Shortcuts* take advantage of ready-made ingredients that cut down on time spent on shopping, prepping, and cooking. Jarred sauces, refrigerated biscuits, rotisserie chickens, taco seasoning packets, and premade pie crusts are just a few of the items I've come across that will let you zip through the express lane so you can get cooking.

Ready-to-use means more than just spice blends and cake mixes. Think about how much has changed in your produce department. There are grab-and-go bags and boxes of washed and mixed salad and other greens; containers of chopped onions, celery, and carrots; and packages of cubed butternut squash and spiral-cut zucchini, carrots, summer squash, and beet noodles, as well as bags of cauliflower rice. Cut-up pineapples, kiwis, mangos, and melons are ready for snacking, for making smoothies, and adding to desserts and salads. (Recipes that call for supermarket-shortcut ingredients are indicated by SUPERMARKETSHORTCUTS. You'll find a list of all of these ingredients starting on page xix.) Even if a recipe in this book doesn't use one of these specific supermarket shortcuts, you can bank on the fact that it will still be incredibly easy and fast.

So now not only can you take advantage of supermarket shortcuts, but also—wait for it—every recipe uses no more than ten ingredients, and some have even fewer.

The other bit of good news is that many of the recipes can be made ahead and frozen. Perfect for busy school-day mornings, Sausage and Pimento Cheese Biscuit Pockets just need to be reheated for a few minutes. Once frozen Buffalo

Chicken Meatballs are reheated, pour some blue cheese dressing into a bowl and watch them disappear. Since Meatball Lasagna is made with jarred tomato sauce, frozen meatballs, and no-boil lasagna noodles, it makes sense to double the recipe and freeze one. That way, there's always a main course in the house.

Time-saving, cutting-edge appliances also continue to make our lives easier. A pressure cooker can turn out mac 'n' cheese in just six minutes, or Pork Chops with Cherry Preserves and Apples can quietly bubble away in the slow cooker while you're busy doing other things. With an air fryer, you can cook Beef Empanadas, Fried Rice, and even Apple-Blueberry Cobbler with no oil or fat—all in record time and with easy cleanup.

Using shortcuts like these keep comfort foods comforting, and the whole process happens a lot quicker. Give yourself a break; not everything has to be made from scratch. Whether it's prepackaged ingredients or a revolutionary appliance that gets the job done more easily, you now have permission to take shortcuts. That way you and yours can spend more time talking at the table instead of getting the food there!

As I've shared with you on my TV show and in previous cookbooks, my mom and grandmothers taught me that meals should be balanced, delicious, and time-saving. They also instilled in me that much of the joy of cooking is about the joy of sharing food with others. *Comfort Food Shortcuts* allows you to spend less time cooking and more time with your family and friends.

For these twenty-five years, I've loved sharing those traditions with you, my foodie friends. So, let's keep cooking together, keep food real and comforting, and keep on enjoying our busy lives.

David's Supermarket Shortcuts

AT THE END OF MANY RECIPES, YOU'LL FIND ONE OR MORE SUGGESTIONS FOR INgredients that will make your comfort cooking easier and quicker. While some of these, like frozen vegetables and panko, may be pantry staples for you, others may not, so I've also put together this handy list for your convenience.

BAKING
Chocolate and strawberry cake mixes

Jiffy Corn Muffin Mix

Graham cracker pie crust and individual
    tartlet shells

Pancake mix

BREAD
English muffins

Flatout Pizza Crusts, Artisan Thin
    Crust Flatbreads

Panko

Stuffing cubes

Texas toasts

CANS, JARS, AND BOXES
Alfredo sauce

Baked beans

Barbecue sauce

Beets

Brown gravy

Cheez Whiz Original Cheese Dip

Chow mein noodles

Condensed Cheddar cheese soup

Condensed cream of chicken soup

Condensed cream of mushroom soup

Condensed French onion soup

Evaporated milk

French-fried onions

Honey-roasted peanuts

Instant espresso coffee granules

Jarred salsa

Kool-Aid Lemonade Unsweetened
  Drink Mix

Lemon-lime soft drink

Low-sodium beef, chicken, and
  vegetable broths

Marinara sauce

Marinated and quartered artichoke

Marshmallow Fluff

Mexican salsa verde

Pickled jalapeños

Pimiento-stuffed green olives

Pizza sauce

Pineapple chunks

Pitted cherries

Quick-cooking grits

Refried beans

RO*TEL Diced Tomatoes and Green
  Chilies

Sliced peaches

Spam

Sweetened condensed milk

Taco sauce

Vodka sauce

Whipped cream

CONDIMENTS AND DRESSINGS

Apricot preserves

Balsamic glaze

Balsamic vinaigrette

Blue cheese dressing

Buffalo wing sauce

Cherry preserves

Chocolate syrup

Dill pickle relish

Hoisin sauce

Honey mustard sauce

Hot sauce

Italian vinaigrette

Key lime juice

Mirin

Oyster sauce

Peanut butter–chocolate spread

Ranch dressing

Sriracha

Stir-fry sauce

Sweet chili sauce

Teriyaki sauce

Thai red curry paste

Thousand Island dressing

CEREALS, COOKIES, AND SNACKS

Biscotti

Chocolate curls

Nabisco Famous Chocolate Wafers

Honey Bunches of Oats®

Mini pretzels

Shelled pistachios

DRY SEASONINGS AND SPICES

Cajun seasoning

Chili seasoning

Fajita seasoning

French onion soup mix

Garam masala

Italian seasoning

Lemon and pepper seasoning

Mexican seasoning

Montreal Steak Seasoning

Old Bay Seasoning

Pork gravy mix

Ranch dressing

Smoked paprika

Taco seasoning

FROZEN FOODS

Asian stir-fry vegetables

Breaded chicken cutlets

Broccoli

Corn kernels

Diced frozen hash browns

Gnocchi

Green beans

Leaf spinach

Lima beans

Mango cubes

Mixed vegetables

Nondairy whipped topping

Onion, red bell pepper, and green bell
 pepper stir-fry mix

Pancakes

Peas

Peas and carrots

Pie crust

Pineapple chunks

Potstickers

Shredded frozen hash browns

Spinach

Strawberry ice cream

Waffles

POTATOES, PASTA, AND RICE

Instant mashed potatoes

Instant or ready rice

No-boil lasagna noodles

Soba noodles

PREPARED FOODS

Precooked ham steak

Precooked pulled pork

Rotisserie chicken

PRODUCE

Butternut squash cubes

Cauliflower

Cauliflower rice

Coleslaw mix

Peeled garlic cloves

Pomegranate seeds

Spiral-cut zucchini noodles

REFRIGERATED FOODS

Canned whipped cream

Cherry juice cocktail

Chicken drumettes and wingettes

Cooked shrimp

Egg roll wrappers

Feta crumbles

Garlic-and-herbs-spreadable cheese

Hard-boiled eggs

Mascarpone

Meat loaf mix

Velveeta

Nondairy whipped topping

Pepperoni Minis

Pesto

Pie crust

Pillsbury Original Crescent Rolls

Pimiento cheese spread

Precooked breakfast sausage

Refrigerated Crusty French Loaf

Refrigerated Biscuits

Refrigerated pie crust

Shredded mozzarella

Spring salad mix

Turkey bacon

Turkey sausage

Appetizers

WHEN FRIENDS OR FAMILY COME TO MY HOUSE, WE SPEND TIME TOGETHER laughing, sharing stories, enjoying one another's company, and of course, eating. There's no better way to get the evening started than with some quick and easy appetizers. Too often, we tend to rely on the same old cheese-and-cracker platter or bowls of nuts and olives. Instead, take advantage of my supermarket shortcuts to put together some creative appetizers and snacks in no time. And they can be great conversation starters, too. Make-ahead Million Dollar Dip or Pepperoni-Stuffed Cheesy Breadsticks are no-fuss bites when entertaining at dinner parties and holiday gatherings.

I've also included two seasonal beverages for adults to enjoy. The cooling Summer Sangria is made with white wine, orange-flavored liqueur, and seasonal fruits like watermelon and berries. The Winter Punch includes pears and warm spices, such as cinnamon, star anise, and fresh ginger.

If the kids ask, "When will dinner be ready?" put together some Antipasto Kebabs or Crazy for Caprese Flatbreads to hold them over.

Million Dollar Dip

I've been to many potluck dinners and parties where this dip is always the first thing to disappear. With just a handful of easy-to-find ingredients, the dip comes together in fewer than five minutes. It would be easy to eat this favorite by the spoonful, but I suggest crackers, tortilla or pita chips, or vegetables as dippers instead.

MAKES 4 CUPS

8 ounces bacon, chopped

¾ cup (6 ounces) mayonnaise

¾ cup (6 ounces) sour cream

1 8-ounce package whipped cream cheese, at room temperature

¾ teaspoon freshly ground black pepper

2 cups (8 ounces) shredded sharp Cheddar

½ cup chopped scallions, plus 1 tablespoon sliced scallions

3 garlic cloves, minced

Cook the bacon in a skillet over medium heat until crisp, 12 to 15 minutes. Drain the bacon on a paper towel–lined plate.

Put the mayonnaise, sour cream, cream cheese, and pepper in the bowl of an electric mixer and beat until creamy. Using a spatula, fold in the shredded Cheddar, the ½ cup chopped scallions, garlic, and bacon until fully incorporated.

The dip can be served immediately garnished with the 1 tablespoon sliced scallions or refrigerated for 2 days. Bring to room temperature about 1½ hours before serving.

Philly Cheesesteak Dip

Put some Philadelphians in a room and the talk invariably turns to two topics: the Eagles, who won the 2018 Super Bowl, and where to find the city's best cheesesteak. This beloved sandwich is made with thinly sliced grilled steak, onions, and bell peppers. Cheese is melted on top and then everything is piled onto a soft, oblong roll. While I do love my cheesesteaks, I thought, "Why not turn all that goodness into a warm dip?" Serve with crunchy, salty tortilla chips; pretzel sticks; or some frozen prebaked soft pretzels that quickly warm up in the oven. No matter what team you root for, this dip is a winner.

MAKES 6 CUPS

1 tablespoon olive oil

1 cup chopped yellow onions

1 green bell pepper, seeded and chopped

1 red bell pepper, seeded and chopped

1 pound cheesesteak meat, frozen and cut into 2-inch pieces (frozen meat is thin, so it will be easy to slice)

1 tablespoon Worcestershire sauce

½ teaspoon freshly ground black pepper

1 15-ounce jar Cheez Whiz Original Cheese Dip, at room temperature

1 8-ounce package cream cheese, cut into 1-inch pieces, at room temperature

8 ounces Velveeta, cut into 1-inch pieces, at room temperature

Heat the olive oil in a large pot over medium heat. Add the onions and bell peppers and sauté until tender, 5 to 7 minutes. Stir in the frozen meat, Worcestershire, and pepper. Cover and cook, stirring occasionally, until the meat is no longer pink, 8 to 10 minutes.

Add the Cheez Whiz, cream cheese, and Velveeta and cook, stirring constantly, until all the cheeses are melted and the mixture is warm. Pour into a bowl and serve with dippers. This dip is best when served the same day it's made.

Dill Pickle Dip

When I was a little boy, I loved to fish a crunchy dill pickle from the glass jar, sometimes chasing the last one around with a fork. All those great tangy, salty, and vinegary flavors are combined in this simple dip. People go crazy for this! Serve with ridged potato chips; they're stronger and hold more dip. Caution: You will most likely lick the bowl.

MAKES 3 CUPS

1 8-ounce package whipped cream cheese, at room temperature
¼ cup (2 ounces) sour cream
2 cups diced dill pickles
¼ cup diced red onion
¼ cup pickle juice

1 garlic clove, minced
1 tablespoon plus 1 teaspoon fresh dill leaves
1 teaspoon freshly ground black pepper

Put the cream cheese and sour cream into the bowl of an electric mixer. Beat on medium speed until creamy. Using a spatula, fold in the pickles, onion, pickle juice, garlic, the 1 tablespoon dill leaves, and pepper until fully incorporated. Spoon into a serving dish, cover, and refrigerate for at least 6 hours or overnight. Garnish with the remaining 1 teaspoon dill leaves before serving. The dip does not keep more than 1 day.

Crazy for Caprese Flatbreads

Yes, I am! Insalata Caprese (salad from the Isle of Capri), made with the ripest tomatoes, the freshest mozzarella, the brightest green basil leaves, and some good extra-virgin olive oil, is my favorite summer salad. When entertaining a crowd, I find it easier to pile the ingredients on prebaked flatbreads and then cut them into serving pieces. If you don't have time to make the pesto, you can certainly use premade sauce.

MAKES 6 SERVINGS

3 cups (about 1¼ ounces) lightly packed fresh basil leaves

2 garlic cloves, peeled

⅓ cup (1½ ounces) grated Parmigiano-Reggiano

½ teaspoon plus ¼ teaspoon freshly ground black pepper

¼ teaspoon kosher salt

¼ cup extra-virgin olive oil

3 Flatout Pizza Crusts, Artisan Thin Crust Flatbreads

1½ cups (6 ounces) shredded mozzarella

2 ripe tomatoes, thinly sliced

Heat the oven to 400°F. Line a sheet pan with aluminum foil.

To make the pesto, put the basil, garlic, Parmigiano-Reggiano, the ½ teaspoon pepper, and the salt into a food processor and pulse until roughly chopped, 6 to 8 times. While the machine is running, slowly add the olive oil in a steady stream until a thick paste forms.

Arrange the flatbreads on the prepared sheet pan. Bake until lightly crisp, 4 to 5 minutes. Remove the flatbreads from the oven and evenly spread the pesto over them. Sprinkle ½ cup mozzarella over each flatbread and evenly distribute the tomato slices on top of the flatbreads. Sprinkle each with the remaining ¼ teaspoon of pepper. Bake until the tomatoes are soft and the cheese is melted, about 15 minutes. Let cool for 2 minutes before slicing and serving.

 SUPERMARKETSHORTCUT

Flatout Pizza Crusts, Artisan Thin Crust Flatbreads

Tex-Mex Skillet Nachos

For successful nachos, put half of the cooked beef mixture in the skillet and top with some chips, and then repeat and top with cheese before baking.

MAKES 8 SERVINGS

1 10-ounce can RO*TEL Diced Tomatoes and Green Chilies, drained
½ cup chopped fresh cilantro
½ cup (4 ounces) sour cream
2 tablespoons fresh lime juice
12 ounces ground beef

1½ cups frozen chopped onions and peppers
1 15-ounce can black beans, drained and rinsed
1 8-ounce jar medium taco sauce
1 8-ounce bag tortilla chips
2 cups (8 ounces) shredded pepper Jack

Heat the oven to 400°F.

Combine the canned tomatoes and chilies and cilantro in a bowl. In a separate bowl, whisk together the sour cream and lime juice. Set bowls aside.

Put the ground beef and frozen onions and peppers in a large ovenproof skillet over medium heat. Cook, stirring occasionally, until the meat is no longer pink, 5 to 6 minutes. Stir in the beans and taco sauce. Reduce the heat to medium-low and cook until heated through, about 5 minutes.

Remove half of the beef-bean mixture from the skillet to a bowl. Put the tortilla chips on top of the beef-bean mixture in the skillet. Put the reserved beef-bean mixture on top of the tortilla chips. Sprinkle the cheese on top.

Bake until the cheese is melted, 5 to 6 minutes. Remove from the oven, drizzle with the sour cream sauce, and top with the tomato mixture.

 SUPERMARKETSHORTCUTS

RO*TEL Diced Tomatoes and Green Chilies • taco sauce

Antipasto Kebabs

A colorful, eye-catching, and ready-in-no-time appetizer doesn't get any easier than these no-cook kebabs. Sliced prosciutto, grape tomatoes, mild pepperoncini, jarred artichoke hearts, and small mozzarella balls (called *ciliegine*) are arranged on 8-inch-long wooden skewers and piled onto platters, then drizzled with balsamic glaze.

Set up an assembly line and let the kids pitch in. Put an empty glass on the table so guests have a place to put their used skewers. I'm not sure which I love more: that every bite offers a new flavor or that there are no dishes to wash.

MAKES 12 SERVINGS

24 small fresh mozzarella balls

24 marinated and quartered
    artichoke hearts from a jar,
    liquid reserved

24 red grape tomatoes

24 thin slices prosciutto

12 pepperoncini

24 fresh basil leaves

12 8-inch wooden skewers

3 tablespoons balsamic glaze

Put the mozzarella balls, artichoke hearts, tomatoes, and ⅓ cup of the artichoke liquid in a bowl. Toss gently to coat all of the ingredients. Refrigerate and marinate for 1 hour.

Assemble by alternating the marinated ingredients, prosciutto, pepperoncini, and basil leaves on the skewers in any order you wish. Arrange the skewers on a platter and drizzle with the balsamic glaze before serving.

SUPERMARKETSHORTCUTS

marinated and quartered artichoke hearts • balsamic glaze

Buffalo Chicken Meatballs with Blue Cheese Dip

These one-bite delights have all the great flavors of Buffalo chicken wings, but without the bones. Ground chicken and bread crumbs are shaped into mini meatballs, then simmered in Buffalo wing sauce. The meatballs absorb the flavors of the sauce, making every bite warm and spicy.

MAKES ABOUT 40 MEATBALLS

1 cup bottled blue cheese dressing

¾ cup minced celery

2 pounds ground chicken

¾ cup plain dry bread crumbs

2 large eggs, lightly beaten

1½ cups bottled Buffalo wing sauce

2 tablespoons cornstarch

¼ cup thinly sliced scallions

Combine the dressing and celery in a bowl to make a blue cheese dip. Cover and refrigerate until needed.

Combine the chicken, bread crumbs, and eggs in a bowl. Using a 1-inch ice cream scoop, shape the mixture into 40 meatballs.

Put the Buffalo wing sauce and ½ cup water in a large sauté pan; add the meatballs and cover. Bring to a boil, reduce to medium-low heat, and simmer until the meatballs are cooked through, about 15 minutes, gently stirring halfway through.

In a small bowl, whisk together the cornstarch and 2 tablespoons water until smooth. Increase the heat under the meatballs to high and add the cornstarch mixture. Bring the sauce to a boil and cook for 1 minute, stirring often.

Serve hot, with the sauce, garnished with scallions and the dip.

SUPERMARKETSHORTCUTS

blue cheese dressing • Buffalo wing sauce

Sheet Pans

The first step in many of my recipes is to heat the oven to the required temperature, followed by instructions to "Line a sheet pan with aluminum foil." A sheet pan is a four-sided flat rectangular pan with rolled edges on all sides, sometimes called a rimmed baking sheet, while a baking sheet has just upturned edges. Sheet pans come in various dimensions, but my go-to sizes are 9 x 13 inches and 13 x 18 inches and are in constant use in my kitchen. I use them to layer and bake the Mexican Tortilla Stack and oven Barbecued Chicken Thighs and roast vegetables.

Purchase sturdy sheet pans and they will last a long time. Lining a sheet pan with aluminum foil or parchment paper makes cleanup a snap.

Pepperoni-Stuffed Cheesy Breadsticks

The ease and magic of refrigerated bread doughs allows us to take America's favorite pizza flavors and roll them into delicious party or meal starters—add a jarred marinara sauce or pizza sauce for dipping.

MAKES 8 SERVINGS

2 11-ounce cans refrigerated Crusty French Loaf
48 (about 3.2 ounces) pepperoni slices
8 mozzarella string cheese sticks

3 tablespoons unsalted butter
1 teaspoon garlic salt
¾ teaspoon Italian seasoning
Pizza sauce, for dipping

Heat the oven to 425°F. Line a sheet pan with aluminum foil.

Unfold the bread dough from one can and place on a work surface. Cut into 4 rectangles measuring 5½ x 6 inches. Place 6 pepperoni slices on the longer side closest to you, then place 1 string cheese stick on top. Fold the dough over, carefully stretching it over the filling to cover it. Then roll the dough like a jelly roll. Pinch the dough to seal all the seams (top and sides). Place the rolled breadsticks on the prepared sheet pan. Using the tip of a paring knife, make 4 small slits in the dough to allow steam to escape. Repeat with the other can of bread and the remaining pepperoni and cheese.

Melt the butter in a saucepan, then stir in the garlic salt and Italian seasoning. Brush the butter mixture evenly over the breadsticks. Bake until golden brown, 15 to 18 minutes. Serve with the pizza sauce, for dipping.

 SUPERMARKETSHORTCUTS

refrigerated Crusty French Loaf • string cheese sticks • Italian seasoning • pizza sauce

Summer Sangria

Most people tend to make sangria with red wine, but when hosting an outdoor dinner party in the summer, I like to offer my guests this colorful sangria with white wine, white grape juice, and orange liqueur. Add the fruit and refrigerate for a few hours. To keep the sangria chilled, frozen mango pieces are added to the glasses before pouring.

MAKES 6 SERVINGS

1 bottle (750 ml) Pinot Grigio or other dry white wine

2 cups white grape juice

½ cup orange-flavored liqueur, such as Grand Marnier or Cointreau

½ cup watermelon cubes

½ cup sliced fresh strawberries

½ cup fresh raspberries

½ cup fresh blueberries

2 cups frozen mango cubes

torn mint leaves

Pour the wine, grape juice, and orange liqueur into a large pitcher and stir well. Add the watermelon, strawberries, raspberries, and blueberries. Refrigerate for 3 hours. Add the frozen mango and mint to the glasses before serving.

 SUPERMARKETSHORTCUT

frozen mango cubes

Winter Punch

Move aside, eggnog! Make room for a warming punch that is perfect for all your winter gatherings. Pear juice is infused with cinnamon, star anise, and ginger, then combined with white wine. (Look for star anise in the spice or Asian foods aisles.) Orange slices, pineapple pieces, and ruby red pomegranate seeds add festive colors. The whole thing comes to life when sparkling wine is added. It's all the flavors of the holidays poured into a glass.

MAKES 6 SERVINGS

3 cups pear juice

4 cinnamon sticks

2 star anise

2 tablespoons chopped fresh ginger

1 cup chilled Sauvignon Blanc

½ navel orange, thinly sliced

½ cup pomegranate seeds

1½ cups frozen pineapple chunks

1 bottle (750 ml) dry sparkling wine, such as Prosecco

Put the pear juice, cinnamon sticks, star anise, and ginger into a small saucepan. Bring to a boil, then reduce the heat to a simmer and cook for 30 minutes. Refrigerate the mixture until chilled.

Strain the pear-spice mixture through a fine-mesh strainer. Discard the spices. Pour the pear-spice mixture into a large pitcher. Stir in the white wine, orange slices, and pomegranate seeds. Just before serving, add the frozen pineapple and sparkling wine to the pitcher and stir well.

 SUPERMARKETSHORTCUTS

pomegranate seeds • frozen pineapple chunks

Be Chill

Just before serving punch or coolers, add some frozen mixed berries, sliced peaches, and pineapple or kiwi and mango chunks to the pitcher or glasses to keep the liquid chilled.

You can also use frozen fruit on skewers for a lovely garnish.

Breakfast and Brunch

WHEN THAT ALARM CLOCK GOES OFF IN THE MORNING, A MILLION THOUGHTS start zooming through your head. What time is that meeting? Lunches packed? Who has to be where after school? Oh, yikes, what about breakfast? Despite the morning rush, we still want to feed our families something filling and nutritious.

This chapter is full of quick-and-easy ideas that go beyond the usual breakfasts, so no one misses the school bus, the car pool, or the commuter train. Make ahead, freeze, and reheat Breakfast Egg Cups and Sausage and Pimento Cheese Biscuit Pockets for weekday breakfasts. For weekends and holidays when morning meals are later and longer, try Breakfast Waffle Bread Pudding with Berries or French Toast Sticks with Cinnamon-Butter Dip. There's no better way to start the day. Or end it. Everyone loves breakfast for dinner. Think about how diners and other casual restaurants offer breakfast all day long. You can do the same with Skillet Breakfast or Turkey Sausage, Croissant, and Egg Casserole.

French Toast Sticks with Cinnamon-Butter Dip

Thick, square Texas toasts are sliced into long strips, then dipped into eggs and coated with crunchy cereal before frying. Served with a buttery, cinnamon-y, maple-y dipping sauce, these French toast sticks taste like cinnamon donuts.

MAKES 4 SERVINGS

Dip

8 tablespoons (1 stick) unsalted butter, softened
¼ cup maple syrup
2 teaspoons ground cinnamon

French Toast Sticks

2 large eggs
½ cup half-and-half
½ teaspoon pure vanilla extract
3½ cups finely crushed Honey Bunches of Oats®
3 tablespoons unsalted butter
4 slices plain Texas toast, cut into 1-inch sticks
Confectioners' sugar

To make the dip, mix together the butter, maple syrup, and cinnamon in a bowl. Set aside.

To make the French toast sticks, in a shallow bowl, whisk together the eggs, half-and-half, and vanilla. Place the crushed cereal in a separate shallow bowl.

Melt the butter in a large skillet over medium heat. Dip the bread sticks into the egg mixture, shaking off any excess, then dip into the cereal, pressing gently to coat.

Add the sticks to the skillet and cook until golden brown, about 3 minutes per side.

Serve the French toast sticks warm, dusted with confectioners' sugar, with a small dish of cinnamon-butter dip alongside.

 SUPERMARKETSHORTCUTS

Honey Bunches of Oats® • Texas toast

Bananas Foster Pancakes

Bananas Foster was created at Brennan's, the famed New Orleans restaurant. The bananas are sautéed in brown sugar and rum, then everything is dramatically flambéed tableside and topped with a scoop of ice cream. I removed the danger of flames but kept all of those great flavors. Starting with frozen pancakes means you're already halfway there. If making these for kids, replace the rum with an equal amount of apple, white grape, or orange juice.

MAKES 4 SERVINGS

8 4-inch frozen pancakes, thawed
½ cup (1 stick) unsalted butter
½ cup (packed) light brown sugar
1 teaspoon ground cinnamon
⅓ cup dark rum

½ teaspoon banana extract
4 bananas, peeled and sliced into
    ¼-inch-thick rounds
½ cup chopped toasted walnuts
    (optional)

Bake the pancakes in the oven or in the microwave according to the package instructions.

Melt the butter, sugar, and cinnamon in a skillet over low heat. Stir constantly until the sugar dissolves, about 4 minutes. Increase the heat to medium, stir in the rum and banana extract, and cook until the sauce thickens, 3 to 4 minutes.

Add the bananas and cook, stirring gently, until they are soft but still hold their shape, 3 to 4 minutes. Pour the banana syrup over the pancakes and top with toasted walnuts, if desired.

SUPERMARKETSHORTCUT

frozen pancakes

Breakfast Waffle Bread Pudding with Berries

Who said bread pudding is just for dessert? Prebaked and frozen waffles cut your prep time in half. Slice the waffles into pieces and layer them in a baking dish. A quick custard sauce of beaten eggs and half-and-half is poured over the top before the dish goes into the oven. Once baked, each portion is topped with a big spoonful of mixed berries tossed with maple syrup.

MAKES 8 SERVINGS

Vegetable oil spray
12 frozen buttermilk waffles, cut into quarters
2 cups half-and-half
6 large eggs
4 tablespoons (½ stick) unsalted butter, melted

¼ cup (packed) light brown sugar
⅔ cup plus ⅓ cup maple syrup
1 tablespoon pure vanilla extract
2 teaspoons ground cinnamon
2 cups mixed fresh berries

Heat the oven to 350°F. Coat a 9 x 13-inch baking dish with vegetable oil spray. Put the cut-up waffles into the prepared dish.

Whisk together the half-and-half, eggs, butter, brown sugar, the ⅔ cup maple syrup, the vanilla, and cinnamon in a bowl. Pour the custard evenly over the waffles and press down to make sure all the waffles are fully coated.

Bake until golden brown and a knife inserted 2½ inches from the edge of the baking dish comes out clean, 45 to 50 minutes.

Toss the berries with the remaining ⅓ cup maple syrup. Top each bread pudding serving with the berry-syrup mixture.

SUPERMARKETSHORTCUT

frozen waffles

Bread and Chocolate

This is what decadent breakfast dreams are made of. A blend of cream cheese and butter is spread on a loaf of egg bread that is not quite sliced all the way through. Then a square of chocolate is tucked between the slices, and the whole loaf is baked until the chocolate becomes soft and velvety smooth. A cup of coffee or a glass of milk is all that's needed to wash it down.

MAKES 10 TO 12 SERVINGS

1 8-ounce package cream cheese, at room temperature

6 tablespoons (¾ stick) unsalted butter, softened

3 tablespoons honey

2 teaspoons pure vanilla extract

1 16- to 22-ounce loaf challah or brioche bread

4 ounces bittersweet chocolate (60% cacao), broken into pieces

Heat the oven to 350°F. Line a sheet pan with aluminum foil.

Put the cream cheese, butter, honey, and vanilla in the bowl of an electric mixer. Beat until the mixture is smooth and creamy, 2 to 3 minutes.

Using a serrated knife, cut the bread vertically into 1-inch slices ¾ of the way through the loaf, leaving a ½-inch uncut portion at the bottom.

Arrange the bread on the prepared pan. With a small spatula, spread the cream cheese mixture evenly between the bread slices. Insert pieces of chocolate between the bread slices. Bake until the cream cheese mixture is gooey and the chocolate is melted, 15 to 17 minutes. Let the bread rest for 10 minutes before serving.

Turkey Sausage, Croissant, and Egg Casserole

When I prepare this make-ahead casserole, I usually bake two and freeze one for future use. Just pop it in the oven while making coffee, cutting up some fruit, and setting the table. Pick up a bag of fresh croissants and some pre-cooked turkey sausage, or use your leftover breakfast sausage.

MAKES 8 SERVINGS

Vegetable oil spray
2 cups half-and-half
8 large eggs
1 teaspoon kosher salt
1 teaspoon freshly ground black pepper

6 large croissants (1 pound, 2 ounces), cut into 1-inch chunks
1 9.6-ounce package fully cooked turkey sausage links, cut into ¼-inch rounds
1½ cups plus ½ cup shredded extra sharp Cheddar

Heat the oven to 350°F. Coat a 9 x 13-inch baking dish with vegetable oil spray.

Whisk the half-and-half, eggs, salt, and pepper together in a bowl. Add the croissant pieces, turkey sausage, and the 1½ cups Cheddar. Gently toss the mixture until combined.

Pour and evenly distribute the mixture into the prepared baking dish. Evenly sprinkle the remaining ½ cup Cheddar on top. Bake for 45 minutes, until golden brown and a knife inserted 2½ inches from the edge of the dish comes out clean.

SUPERMARKETSHORTCUT
turkey sausage

Sausage and Pimento Cheese Biscuit Pockets

These savory breakfast pockets are fun and easy. Best of all, since they have no eggs, these handheld morning treats can be made ahead, reheated, and then wrapped in a napkin for breakfast as you head out the door to start your day.

MAKES 8 SERVINGS

Vegetable oil spray
1 can (16.3 ounces) Grands!™ Flaky Layers Buttermilk Biscuits
Flour, for dusting the work surface

⅓ cup pimento cheese spread
1 cup chopped precooked breakfast sausage
1 large egg

Heat the oven to 375°F. Line a sheet pan with aluminum foil and lightly coat it with vegetable oil spray.

Remove the biscuits from the can. On a lightly floured surface, use a rolling pin to roll each biscuit into a 6-inch circle. Place 2 teaspoons of pimento cheese in the center of each circle, then top each with 2 tablespoons cooked sausage. Fold the edges over and press closed. Place the biscuit pockets on the prepared pan and press the edges with a fork to seal tightly.

Whisk together the egg and 1 teaspoon water in a bowl until combined. Brush the top of each pocket with the egg wash. Make a small slit with a knife tip on the top of each one to allow the steam to escape. Bake for 20 to 22 minutes or until golden brown. Cool on a rack for no more than 5 minutes; they should be eaten warm.

Individually wrap any leftovers in plastic wrap, refrigerate, and reheat in the microwave for 2 to 3 minutes.

 SUPERMARKETSHORTCUTS

refrigerated biscuits • pimento cheese spread • precooked breakfast sausage

Breakfast Egg Cups

Do you know the muffin pan? That one in your cabinet? That handy-dandy pan can be used for so much more than just muffins and cupcakes. Using refrigerated pie crust, you can easily make single-portion egg cups for breakfast and brunch. Once made, cover and store them in the refrigerator for a day or two and reheat them in the oven.

MAKES 8 SERVINGS

Vegetable oil spray

1 14.1-ounce package refrigerated pie crusts, softened as directed on box

4 thin slices deli ham, cut into quarters

8 tablespoons garlic-and-herb spreadable cheese, such as Boursin, at room temperature

½ teaspoon freshly ground black pepper

8 large eggs

½ teaspoon kosher salt

2 tablespoons chopped fresh chives

Heat the oven to 375°F. Put an oven rack in the lower third of the oven. Coat 8 cups of a muffin pan with vegetable oil spray.

Unroll a pie crust and trim about 1 inch per side of the edges to make an 8½-inch square, then cut the dough into 4 squares. Repeat with the remaining pie crust. There will be a total of 8 squares.

Tightly press the sides and bottoms of the squares into the prepared muffin cups. Put 2 pieces of ham in each muffin cup. Spoon 1 tablespoon of the cheese into each muffin, pressing it to cover the bottom. Sprinkle each with a few grinds of pepper. Crack an egg into each muffin cup and sprinkle with salt.

Bake until the crust is golden brown and cooked through, about 25 minutes. Remove from the oven. Gently turn out the egg cups and sprinkle with chives.

 SUPERMARKETSHORTCUTS

frozen pie crust • garlic and herb spreadable cheese

Loaded Breakfast Hash Browns

I rarely have time in my weekly schedule to go out for breakfast. But when I do, you can bet that I head to the local diner for a big side of hash browns with my eggs. At home, my version of this classic takes advantage of frozen hash brown potatoes. And because hash is, well, hash, you can add whatever you like to it. Try some leftover bacon, sausage, and mushrooms, with a fried egg on top.

MAKES 4 SERVINGS

1 tablespoon vegetable oil

1 red bell pepper, seeded and chopped

½ cup chopped yellow onion

2 garlic cloves, minced

8 ounces ham steak, cut into ¼-inch pieces

3 cups shredded frozen hash browns

1 tablespoon minced fresh thyme leaves or 1 teaspoon dried thyme

1 teaspoon kosher salt

¾ teaspoon freshly ground black pepper

¼ cup chopped scallions

Heat the oil in a large skillet over medium heat. Add the bell pepper, onion, and garlic and sauté until the onion is softened, 4 to 5 minutes. Stir in the ham, hash browns, thyme, salt, and pepper. Cover with a lid and cook until the potatoes are golden brown, 15 to 18 minutes. Using a spatula, turn the potatoes in sections just once about halfway through the cooking process. Sprinkle on the scallions and serve immediately.

 SUPERMARKETSHORTCUTS

precooked ham steak • shredded frozen hash browns

Skillet Breakfast

This hearty one-dish wonder traveled from North Africa to Israel to brunch menus around the world. I decided to take this classic on a southern detour by adding a layer of Cheddar grits on the bottom of the skillet. Once the tomato sauce is added, the eggs are nestled into the skillet. Pop the whole thing in the oven and bake until the eggs are cooked as you like them. Bring the skillet to the table and then dish out your servings. Accompany with toasted pita wedges, English muffins, or crusty bread so you don't miss a drop. If you love your eggs with a little heat, feel free to add some hot sauce.

MAKES 4 SERVINGS

⅓ cup chopped yellow onion

¼ cup quick-cooking grits

¼ teaspoon plus ¼ teaspoon freshly ground black pepper

¼ teaspoon kosher salt

1¼ cups (5 ounces) shredded extra-sharp white Cheddar

⅓ cup tomato sauce

4 large eggs

1 tablespoon chopped fresh chives

Heat the oven to 375°F.

Bring 1 cup water to a boil in a saucepan. Add the onion, grits, the ¼ teaspoon pepper, and the salt. Stir to combine, then reduce the heat to medium-low and cook until thick, stirring occasionally, 5 to 7 minutes. Stir in the Cheddar and continue to cook until the cheese is melted, about 1 minute.

Pour the grits into an ovenproof skillet. Gently spoon on the tomato sauce. Carefully crack the eggs into the skillet, leaving room between each. Season with the remaining ¼ teaspoon pepper. Bake until the eggs are set but the yolks are runny, 16 to 18 minutes. Garnish with chives before serving.

SUPERMARKETSHORTCUT
quick-cooking grits

BETA Breakfast Bowl

Breakfast bowls let you think outside the cereal box when it comes to your morning meal. The ideas for these all-in-one meals are endless. Some bowls can take a savory grain-based turn, while sweeter versions can start with a scoop of yogurt topped with some fresh fruit, nuts, and flaked coconut. My favorite breakfast bowl includes some chopped bacon (B), scrambled eggs (E), tomatoes (T), and creamy avocado slices (A). When serving these bowls at brunch, I pass a basket of multigrain toast to go alongside.

MAKES 4 SERVINGS

8 large eggs
⅓ cup (2½ ounces) sour cream
½ teaspoon kosher salt
8 strips bacon, cut into 1-inch pieces
½ cup (2 ounces) shredded extra-sharp Cheddar

1 ripe avocado, pitted, peeled, quartered, and sliced
8 grape tomatoes, halved
½ teaspoon freshly ground black pepper

Whisk together the eggs, sour cream, and salt in a bowl.

Cook the bacon in a skillet over medium heat until crisp, 12 to 15 minutes. Remove the bacon to a paper towel–lined plate with a slotted spoon. Leave 2 tablespoons of the bacon fat in the skillet and discard the rest.

Pour the egg mixture into the pan, and using a spatula, cook over medium heat, stirring constantly, until the eggs are scrambled, 3 to 4 minutes.

Divide the scrambled eggs among four bowls and sprinkle the Cheddar over the eggs to melt.

Top each bowl with the avocado slices, tomato halves, cooked bacon, and a few grinds of pepper.

Say Cheese!

Cheddar, Parmigiano-Reggiano, Monterey Jack, and other hard cheeses used in this book are sold by weight, rather than by volume. When it comes to cheese, I believe in buying a chunk and grating or shredding it myself. Potato starch and powdered cellulose are often added to packaged shredded cheeses to prevent them from caking. This also keeps the cheese from melting smoothly and evenly. The only shredded cheese I purchase is mozzarella because its softness makes it difficult to shred. If you're game, however, try shredding it on the large holes of a box grater. Here's a handy chart to help you purchase the right amounts of cheeses for the recipes in *Comfort Food Shortcuts*.

WEIGHT	VOLUME
1 pound cheese	4 cups shredded
8 ounces	2 cups shredded
4 ounces	1 cup shredded
3 ounces	¾ cup shredded
2 ounces	½ cup shredded
1 ounce	¼ cup shredded

Soups and Salads

CHOPPING, SLICING, MINCING, DICING, AND SHREDDING VEGETABLES, HERBS, and other ingredients for soups and salads take up a lot of time. When it comes to soups, most of them need to simmer, rather than boil, for hours over low heat so the vegetables hold together and don't fall apart. Not these soups. You'll be delighted at how quickly they come together with the help of supermarket shortcuts. Once peeled and cubed butternut squash is cooked with pears and seasonings, the mixture is puréed in the same pot with an immersion blender or in the bowl of a standing blender. Add frozen— that's right, frozen—potstickers to broth with vegetables for an instant meal in a bowl.

Already-prepped ingredients found in produce sections make it easy to change up from the same old greens-with-dressing every night to colorful and inspired new salad ideas. A bag of coleslaw mix tossed with a ginger–soy sauce dressing and some peanuts, then topped with crunchy chow mein noodles, goes with stir-fries or grilled meat or fish. Tender roasted and peeled beets, creamy goat cheese, and crunchy candied pistachios add various textures when piled on mixed greens.

Butternut Squash–Pear Soup

When autumn arrives, combine butternut squash and sweet pears to make this velvety, satisfying soup. Puréed to a creamy consistency, this soup is elegant enough to offer as a first course when company is coming. Or pass small cups of this slightly sweet, mostly savory soup as an appetizer. Garnish with some crumbled bacon or a spoonful of crème fraîche.

If you purchase butternut squash that is cut into large chunks, cut them into smaller pieces for faster cooking.

MAKES 6 SERVINGS

3 tablespoons unsalted butter
1½ pounds butternut squash, cut into 1-inch pieces
1 ripe pear, peeled, cored, and cut into pieces
2 teaspoons minced fresh ginger
3 cups low-sodium vegetable broth

1¾ cups pear juice
¾ teaspoon kosher salt
¾ teaspoon freshly ground black pepper
½ cup plain nonfat Greek yogurt
¼ cup chopped walnuts

Melt the butter in a large pot over medium-high heat. Add the squash, pear, and ginger. Cook for 5 minutes, stirring occasionally. Add the broth, pear juice, salt, and pepper. Reduce the heat to medium and cook until the squash is tender, 30 to 35 minutes.

Remove the pot from the heat. Stir in the yogurt. Purée the soup until smooth with an immersion blender or standing blender. Follow the blender instructions when blending hot liquids.

Ladle the soup into bowls and garnish with the chopped walnuts.

SUPERMARKETSHORTCUTS

peeled and cut butternut squash • low-sodium vegetable broth

Mac 'n' Cheese Soup with Ham

I have made it my life's mission to incorporate mac 'n' cheese into a meal whenever possible. So, I took my favorite dish and turned it into a hearty, family-friendly soup that can be on the weeknight table in less than thirty minutes. Hey, Mom and Dad, since there are no green vegetables in the soup, why not pair this with a crunchy salad loaded with chopped carrots and celery?

MAKES 6 TO 8 SERVINGS

1 tablespoon kosher salt

6 ounces (about 1½ cups) small pasta shells

1 tablespoon unsalted butter

1 8-ounce package ham steak, diced

3 cups low-sodium chicken broth

2 10¾-ounce cans condensed Cheddar cheese soup

1 14.5-ounce can petite diced tomatoes

1 teaspoon freshly ground black pepper

2 cups (8 ounces) shredded sharp Cheddar

Bring a large pot of water and the salt to a boil. Add the shells, stir occasionally, and cook until done, 8 to 10 minutes. Drain the shells in a colander, but do not rinse.

In the same pot, melt the butter over medium heat. Add the ham and cook until browned, about 5 minutes, stirring occasionally. Add the broth, condensed soup, tomatoes, and pepper. Cook until heated through, stirring occasionally. Stir in the cooked shells to heat and the Cheddar to melt. Ladle the hot soup into bowls.

 SUPERMARKETSHORTCUTS

precooked ham steak • low-sodium chicken broth • condensed Cheddar cheese soup

Potsticker Soup

Potstickers are small meat-and-vegetable-filled dumplings that have been a favorite of mine ever since I first ordered them at a Chinese restaurant when I was in college. I have since introduced potstickers to hundreds of thousands of people on my TV show. The good news is that you can now find frozen potstickers filled with chicken, pork, shrimp, crab, or vegetables in most grocery stores. While they're great on their own, I often add frozen potstickers to a pot of simmering soup. In a matter of minutes, you'll have this soup on the table faster than you can say, "Where's the take-out menu?"

MAKES 4 SERVINGS

1 tablespoon vegetable oil
⅔ cup shredded carrots
½ cup thinly sliced red bell
   pepper
¼ cup thinly sliced celery
¼ cup plus 3 tablespoons sliced
   scallions

2 teaspoons minced fresh ginger
¾ teaspoon freshly ground black
   pepper
5 cups low-sodium beef broth
2 tablespoons soy sauce
12 frozen potstickers

Heat the oil in a large pot over medium heat. Add the carrots, bell pepper, celery, the ¼ cup scallions, the ginger, and pepper and sauté for 5 minutes. Stir in the broth and soy sauce and bring to a boil. Add the potstickers, reduce the heat, and simmer for 5 to 7 minutes, until the potstickers are heated through.

Ladle into bowls and sprinkle with the 3 tablespoons scallions.

SUPERMARKETSHORTCUTS

low-sodium beef broth • frozen potstickers

Taco Soup

Tacos are popular because there are so many endless combinations, from the fillings (beef, chicken, pork, vegetable) to toppings of all kinds. Why not take some of those same flavors—a packet of taco seasoning and a bag of frozen mixed peppers and onions—and incorporate them into a substantial soup? This is everything we love about tacos, served in a bowl.

MAKES 6 SERVINGS

6 hard taco shells
2 teaspoons olive oil
1 pound lean ground beef
1 16-ounce bag frozen onion, red bell pepper, and green bell pepper stir-fry mix
1 1-ounce packet taco seasoning

½ teaspoon freshly ground black pepper
¼ teaspoon red pepper flakes
4 cups low-sodium beef broth
1 8-ounce can Spanish-style tomato sauce
⅓ cup chopped fresh cilantro

Using your hands, break 4 taco shells into large pieces and put them into a food processor and process until finely ground. Set aside.

Heat the olive oil in a pot over medium-high heat. Add the beef and vegetables. Cook, stirring regularly to break up the beef into smaller pieces, until the meat is cooked through and no longer pink, 7 to 9 minutes. Stir in the taco seasoning, black pepper, and pepper flakes to coat evenly. Stir in the broth, tomato sauce, and the ground taco shells. Bring to a boil, reduce the heat to medium-low, and simmer for 6 to 8 minutes. Stir in the cilantro.

Top each bowl of soup with the remaining taco shells, roughly crushed, and serve.

 SUPERMARKETSHORTCUTS

frozen onion, red bell pepper, and green bell pepper stir-fry mix • taco seasoning • low-sodium beef broth

Zoodle Vegetable Soup

Zoodles are zucchini noodles. Swoodles are sweet potato noodles. Coodles are carrot noodles. Squoodles are squash noodles. There's a whole new vocabulary for spiral-cut vegetables! Certainly, make your own at home if you like, with a spiralizer, although supermarkets now offer all kinds of spiral-cut vegetable noodles. Swirl after swirl, corkscrew after corkscrew, these zoodles in vegetable soup are ideal if you're looking to cut back on carbs. And kids tend to eat more good-for-them foods when vegetables are served in fun and unexpected ways.

MAKES 4 SERVINGS

1 tablespoon olive oil
¾ cup chopped yellow onions
¾ cup chopped carrots
¼ cup chopped celery
3 garlic cloves, minced
4 cups low-sodium vegetable broth

1 teaspoon Italian seasoning
½ teaspoon kosher salt
½ teaspoon freshly ground black pepper
4 cups spiral-cut zucchini (about 4 medium zucchini)

Heat the oil in a large pot over medium heat. Add the onions, carrots, celery, and garlic and sauté for 5 to 6 minutes, until the onions are translucent.

Add the broth, Italian seasoning, salt, and pepper. Bring the soup to a boil, then reduce the heat to a simmer. Cook until the carrots are just soft enough to be pierced with a fork, about 5 minutes. Stir in the zucchini and cook until soft, 2 to 3 minutes. Ladle into bowls and serve immediately.

 SUPERMARKETSHORTCUTS

low-sodium vegetable broth • Italian seasoning • spiral-cut zucchini noodles

Quinoa-Tomato Soup

Originally grown in mountainous regions of South America, quinoa has become so popular that it's now farmed all over the world. Like other grains, quinoa, which is actually a seed, benefits from a quick stove-top toasting in a skillet to bring out its nutty flavor. When this nutritious grain is combined with a rich tomato base, the result is a substantial soup with layers of flavor. I love serving this with my favorite grilled cheese sandwich—a perfect pairing.

MAKES 6 SERVINGS

1 tablespoon olive oil

½ cup quinoa

1 14.5-ounce can diced tomatoes, drained

1 cup chopped yellow onions

⅔ cup chopped celery

1 tablespoon smoked paprika

1½ teaspoons garlic salt

1 teaspoon freshly ground black pepper

6 cups low-sodium chicken broth

⅓ cup chopped fresh cilantro

Heat the oil in a large pot over medium heat. Add the quinoa and toast, stirring frequently, until it turns golden brown and smells nutty, 4 to 6 minutes.

Add the tomatoes, onions, celery, paprika, garlic salt, and pepper. Cook for 5 minutes, stirring occasionally. Stir in the broth and bring to a boil. Reduce the heat to medium and simmer until the quinoa is soft, about 20 minutes. Ladle the soup into bowls and top each with a sprinkle of cilantro.

 **SUPERMARKET**SHORTCUT

low-sodium chicken broth

Smoked Paprika

My mom always garnished her deviled eggs and potato salad with a good sprinkle of sweet paprika. As an ingredient, paprika is the main flavoring in Hungarian goulash and chicken pa- prikash.

In Spain, dried peppers are smoked over wood fires and then ground into paprika, or pi- mentón, as it is called in Spanish. Smoked paprika has a distinct aroma and unmistakable flavor. It is used to make chorizo, is sprinkled over fried eggs and potatoes, and is added to soups and stews. Smoked paprika can be bittersweet, sweet, or hot. Look for it in supermarkets or online. I use sweet smoked paprika in Quinoa-Tomato Soup (page 60) and Mexican Street Corn Off the Cob (page 196). You'll find it in the spice aisle.

Cold Sesame Noodles

If you have a box of spaghetti, some peanut butter, and soy sauce in your pantry, this Chinese restaurant classic comes together in no time. As soon as the noodles are drained and still hot, put them in a bowl and toss with the peanut sauce so it melts quickly and coats all of the spaghetti. If you have any leftovers, refrigerate the noodles, then toss with a tablespoon of warm water to loosen them up before serving. Cold sesame noodles travel well, too. Just put them in a large plastic container with a tight-fitting lid, and before serving give the whole thing a couple of good shakes.

MAKES 8 TO 10 SERVINGS

1 tablespoon kosher salt
1 pound spaghetti
1¼ cups low-sodium chicken broth
¼ cup creamy or chunky peanut
   butter
¼ cup soy sauce
¼ cup hoisin sauce

3 tablespoons rice vinegar
2 tablespoons toasted sesame oil
1½ tablespoons minced fresh
   ginger
⅔ cup thinly sliced scallions
1 tablespoon sesame seeds

Bring a large pot of water and the salt to a boil. Add the spaghetti, stir occasionally, and cook until done. Drain the spaghetti in a colander and put into a bowl.

Put the broth, peanut butter, soy sauce, hoisin sauce, vinegar, sesame oil, and ginger in a saucepan. Bring the mixture to a boil, then lower the heat and cook, whisking occasionally, until the sauce is smooth and heated through, about 1 minute.

Add the sauce to the warm noodles and toss to coat. Let the noodles sit at room temperature for 15 minutes. Garnish with the scallions and sesame seeds just before serving.

SUPERMARKETSHORTCUTS

low-sodium chicken broth • hoisin sauce

Asian Shredded Salad

After work on Sundays, I kick back at home and order in some Chinese food. It's all I can do not to eat all the crispy chow mein noodles before I add them to my soup. Thick or thin, the noodles make a crunchy garnish for this salad, which is easy to put together with coleslaw mix, some peanuts, and a soy sauce and rice vinegar dressing. Serve this as a side with grilled fish, chicken, or steak. You can stir in some shredded rotisserie chicken or cooked and diced shrimp to make this a one-dish meal.

MAKES 8 TO 10 SERVINGS

12 cups coleslaw mix
1 cup honey-roasted peanuts
1 cup chopped fresh cilantro
⅓ cup soy sauce
¼ cup vegetable oil
¼ cup rice vinegar

1 tablespoon minced fresh ginger
1¼ teaspoons freshly ground black pepper
1 teaspoon kosher salt
1 cup chow mein noodles

Combine the coleslaw mix, peanuts, cilantro, soy sauce, oil, vinegar, ginger, pepper, and salt in a bowl. Toss well to combine. When ready to serve, top the slaw with the chow mein noodles.

 SUPERMARKETSHORTCUTS
coleslaw mix • honey-roasted peanuts • chow mein noodles

Panzanella

Toasted bread cubes and cut-up tomatoes are the starring ingredients in this Tuscan summer salad. The tomatoes' juices, vinegar, and good extra-virgin olive oil help to soften the crunchy bread. Toss with some thinly sliced red onions and a good handful of chopped parsley. Enjoy this as a colorful main course, a lunchtime salad, or pair it with grilled sausages, steak, or chicken for dinner.

MAKES 6 SERVINGS

1 12-ounce loaf rustic bread, cut into 1-inch cubes

¼ cup plus 1 tablespoon plus ¼ cup extra-virgin olive oil

½ teaspoon plus ½ teaspoon freshly ground black pepper

4 garlic cloves, minced

2 tablespoons apple cider vinegar

¾ teaspoon kosher salt

1½ pounds multicolored cherry tomatoes, halved

⅓ cup thinly sliced red onion

⅓ cup chopped fresh parsley leaves

Heat a large skillet over medium heat.

Toss the bread cubes with the ¼ cup olive oil and the ½ teaspoon pepper in a bowl. Put the bread in the skillet and toast, stirring occasionally, until golden brown, 8 to 10 minutes. You may need to toast the bread in batches. Put the bread into a serving bowl. Put the 1 tablespoon olive oil and the garlic in the skillet and sauté until fragrant, about 2 minutes.

For the dressing, whisk together the cooked garlic, the remaining ¼ cup olive oil, the remaining ½ teaspoon pepper, the vinegar, and the salt.

Add the tomatoes, onion, parsley, and dressing to the bread cubes and mix well until everything is coated. Serve immediately. The longer the salad sits, the softer the bread will become.

Beets, Goat Cheese, and Candied Pistachios with Greens

I have developed a real affection for beets of all colors and stripes. Yes, there are even candy-striped beets. I was always reluctant to make this favorite of mine at home because beets are hard to peel and their bright colors splatter and stain. Use canned beets or try the vacuum-packed ones in the produce section; they're already cooked and peeled. To make this salad, just slice and arrange the beets on a bed of greens or peppery arugula. Add some orange segments, goat cheese crumbles, toasted nuts, and a simple vinaigrette.

MAKES 4 SERVINGS

¾ cup shelled pistachios

3 tablespoons sugar

⅛ teaspoon cayenne

10 ounces (about 8 cups) spring salad mix

½ cup balsamic vinaigrette

2 15-ounce cans whole beets, drained and cut into 1-inch pieces

2 navel oranges, peeled and segmented

½ cup goat cheese crumbles

Line a dinner plate with parchment paper. Heat a skillet over medium-high heat. Add the pistachios, sugar, 1 tablespoon water, and the cayenne, then cook, stirring occasionally, for 2 minutes. Reduce the heat to medium-low and continue to cook the nuts until they are golden brown and covered with the sugar, 1 to 2 minutes. Spread the nuts in a single layer onto the parchment paper–lined plate to cool.

Combine the salad greens, vinaigrette, and beets in a bowl and toss well. Divide the salad among four plates. Top each serving with the pistachios, orange segments, and crumbled goat cheese.

 SUPERMARKETSHORTCUTS

shelled pistachios • balsamic vinaigrette • cooked beets • goat cheese crumbles

Beef

FOR MOST OF US, A SHORTCUT BEEF DINNER MEANS BURGERS IN A SKILLET OR steaks on the grill, because pot roasts, short ribs, and brisket require many hours in the oven. So what's the secret to making a great beef dinner quickly? Choosing the right meats and using some supermarket shortcuts. A weeknight celebration calls for a beef tenderloin that cooks to perfection in thirty minutes or less. Dress up ground beef by making classic Salisbury Steak with some jarred gravy or preparing chili mac using chili seasoning. Combine ground beef with sausage for a multipurpose meat sauce that can be portioned and frozen to use on pasta or polenta later in the week. If you're hankering for a quick steak, try skirt, a long, thin cut of meat that's done in minutes on the grill or in a grill pan. Top with some red chimichurri, an earthy uncooked sauce of cilantro, garlic, and spices.

To Cook in a Grill Pan

The steaks will have to be cut in half to fit in a grill pan and cooked in batches. Heat the pan over medium-high heat. Brush the steaks with the 1 tablespoon olive oil and season with salt and pepper. Cook the steaks to the desired doneness, about 5 to 6 minutes per side. They will cook faster in the pan than on a grill.

Grilled Skirt Steak
with Red Chimichurri

Skirt steak is an affordable, lean cut that's long and flat. Here it's grilled and served with chimichurri, a no-cook sauce from Argentina. There's a green version (chimichurri verde) as well as a red sauce (chimichurri rojo) like this one. If using a grill pan, cut the steaks in half so they will fit nicely in the pan.

MAKES 4 TO 6 SERVINGS

Chimichurri

½ cup fresh cilantro leaves

3 tablespoons extra-virgin olive oil

3 tablespoons fresh lime juice

1 tablespoon paprika

3 garlic cloves

½ teaspoon ground cumin

¼ teaspoon cayenne

¼ teaspoon salt

¼ teaspoon freshly ground black pepper

Steaks

2 1-pound skirt steaks

1 tablespoon olive oil, plus more for brushing

1 teaspoon salt

1 teaspoon freshly ground black pepper

Heat the grill to high heat.

To make the chimichurri sauce, put the cilantro, 3 tablespoons olive oil, lime juice, paprika, garlic, cumin, cayenne, salt, and pepper in a food processor. Blend until the cilantro is minced, about 5 seconds.

To cook the steaks, brush the steaks with the 1 tablespoon olive oil, then season with the salt and pepper.

Brush the grill grates with oil. Cook the skirt steaks on the grill to desired doneness, 6 to 7 minutes per side for medium-rare. Remove the steaks to a cutting board and allow to rest for 5 minutes. Thinly slice against the grain and serve with the chimichurri sauce.

Beef Stew with Dumplings

This is a take on my mother's chicken and dumplings. Refrigerated biscuits are sliced and dropped into a simmering stew where they rise to the surface and absorb some of the gravy. This would make Mom proud.

MAKES 6 SERVINGS

1 tablespoon vegetable oil

2 pounds beef sirloin steak, trimmed and cut into ½-inch cubes

½ cup all-purpose flour

4 cups low-sodium beef broth

2 10.5-ounce cans condensed French onion soup

2 cups frozen peas and carrots

2 cups frozen cut green beans

3 tablespoons tomato paste

1 teaspoon freshly ground black pepper

½ teaspoon dried thyme

1 16.3-ounce can Grands!™ Flaky Layers Buttermilk Biscuits, cut into quarters

Heat the oil in a large pot over medium-high heat. Add the beef and cook, stirring occasionally, until browned, about 5 minutes. Add the flour and stir to coat the beef. Cook for 3 minutes, stirring occasionally.

Add the broth, condensed soup, peas and carrots, green beans, tomato paste, pepper, and thyme. Bring to a boil, then reduce to medium-low and cover. Cook until the beef is tender when pierced with a fork, 45 to 50 minutes.

Remove the cover and evenly arrange the biscuits on top of the stew. Using the back of a spoon, gently press the biscuits into the stew so they are submerged. Cover and cook until the biscuits are puffy, have doubled in size, and are floating on the surface, about 15 minutes.

SUPERMARKETSHORTCUTS

low-sodium beef broth • condensed French onion soup • frozen peas and carrots • frozen green beens • Grands!™ Flaky Layers Buttermilk Biscuits

Frozen Fruits and Vegetables

I'm a big fan of frozen fruits and vegetables, especially during the winter months when some of my favorites aren't readily available. Frozen fruits and vegetables are processed within hours of harvest, then quickly blanched in hot water to prevent spoiling and immediately frozen, which seals in nutrition. When tightly sealed, frozen fruits and vegetables keep for months and don't spoil like fresh ones. Do use them within several months or else they will lose their color and moisture. Just measure out the amount you need and get cooking. Frozen vegetables rarely require thawing; just pour them frozen into the pot along with the other ingredients.

Meat Lover's Chili Mac

No need to choose between mac 'n' cheese and chili when it comes to this Midwestern stove-top classic. First, the bacon and the beef are quickly cooked in a large stockpot, then the vegetables, elbow macaroni, and beef stock are added. Everything simmers together in one pot for less than thirty minutes. Comfort food made easy just got simpler. Since this makes such a big batch, plan to freeze the leftovers.

MAKES 8 TO 10 SERVINGS

8 ounces thick-sliced bacon, chopped

1 pound lean ground beef

1 red bell pepper, seeded and chopped

1 cup chopped yellow onions

1 28-ounce can crushed tomatoes

1 pound elbow macaroni

3 cups low-sodium beef broth

2 1.25-ounce packages McCormick Chili Seasoning Original

2 cups (8 ounces) shredded Monterey Jack

Put the bacon in a large pot. Turn on the heat to medium-high and cook until the bacon releases some of its fat, about 5 minutes, stirring occasionally. Add the ground beef and cook while breaking it into small pieces, until browned, 6 to 8 minutes. Add the bell pepper and onions and cook until the onions are translucent, 5 to 6 minutes, stirring occasionally. Add the tomatoes, macaroni, beef broth, and seasoning mix. Stir to combine and bring the mixture to a boil, then reduce the heat to medium-low and cover. Cook for 10 minutes, stirring occasionally, or until the pasta is tender but firm to the bite. If necessary, cook for another few minutes until the pasta is done. Ladle the chili mac into bowls and sprinkle on the shredded cheese.

SUPERMARKETSHORTCUTS

low-sodium beef broth • chili seasoning

Teriyaki Rib-Eye Steaks

The rib-eye is one of the juiciest and most flavorful steaks because of the marbled fat throughout. Marinating rib-eyes in teriyaki sauce, mirin, and other seasonings for 8 to 12 hours brings this meat lovers' favorite to a whole new level.

MAKES 6 SERVINGS

1 cup teriyaki sauce
1 cup mirin
⅓ cup (packed) light brown sugar
2 tablespoons minced fresh ginger
5 garlic cloves, minced

4 1-pound boneless beef rib-eye steaks
1 tablespoon vegetable oil
1 tablespoon kosher salt
1 tablespoon freshly ground black pepper

Whisk together the teriyaki sauce, mirin, brown sugar, ginger, and garlic in a bowl. Put the steaks and the teriyaki mixture into a large resealable plastic bag. Seal the bag and toss to coat. Place the bag in a baking dish (to catch any drips) and refrigerate for 8 to 12 hours.

Place an oven rack in the middle of the oven. Heat the broiler to high. Line a sheet pan with aluminum foil.

Remove the steaks from the marinade and pat dry with paper towels. Discard any leftover marinade.

Heat the oil in a large skillet over high heat. Season the steaks with the salt and pepper. Working in batches, two at a time, put the steaks in the skillet and sear on both sides, about 2 minutes per side. Place the seared steaks on the prepared sheet pan and broil to the desired doneness. For medium, the temperature on an instant-read thermometer will read 140°F; for medium-rare, 130°F. When the steaks are cooked, let them rest for 5 minutes before slicing.

SUPERMARKETSHORTCUTS

teriyaki sauce • mirin

Double-Delicious Meat Sauce

Made with ground beef and chopped mild sausage, this meaty, tomato-y sauce has endless uses. Ladle some over your choice of twisty pasta so the sauce gets into the nooks and crannies. You can also layer the sauce in a lasagna. Serve it on polenta or a baked potato. If you want to make it even richer, more like Bolognese, add some heavy cream toward the end. Double or triple the sauce and freeze it in small containers, so dinner is just minutes away.

MAKES 2½ QUARTS

2 28-ounce cans peeled whole tomatoes
1 pound mild Italian sausage
1 pound lean ground beef
1 cup chopped yellow onions
6 garlic cloves, minced
¼ cup tomato paste

1 cup lightly packed fresh basil leaves
1 teaspoon dried oregano
1½ teaspoons freshly ground black pepper
1¼ teaspoons kosher salt

Put the tomatoes and their juice in a large bowl, then crush by hand or with a potato masher. Set aside.

Put the sausage and ground beef in a large pot over medium-high heat. Cook the meats, breaking them into small pieces and stirring occasionally, until browned, 6 to 8 minutes.

Add the onions and garlic and cook for 3 minutes, stirring frequently. Stir in the crushed tomatoes, tomato paste, basil, oregano, pepper, and salt. Reduce the heat to medium and simmer for 25 minutes, stirring occasionally, until fully flavored.

Oooey-Gooey Patty Melts

Say "patty melt," and I take a step back in time and think of old-fashioned diners with endless menus, waitresses who can carry four plates at the same time, and a cook dressed in white who mans the huge griddle. When an order for a patty melt comes at him, he cooks a burger on the griddle, flips it, adds a slice of cheese, and then covers the whole thing with a metal bowl so the cheese will melt. The patty is then placed on toasted rye bread that has been spread with a tangy dressing. Patty melts are easy to make at home and are a nice change from cheeseburgers. Just add some pickles and potato chips to each plate. Watch out, though—if you're eating a patty melt correctly, some of it will definitely drip down your shirt!

MAKES 4 SERVINGS

1 tablespoon vegetable oil

1 large yellow onion, halved and thinly sliced

4 (5 to 6 ounces each) beef burger patties

1 teaspoon kosher salt

1 teaspoon freshly ground black pepper

¾ cup Thousand Island dressing

8 slices rye bread

16 slices Colby Jack

4 tablespoons (½ stick) unsalted butter

Heat the oil in a large skillet over medium-high heat. Add the onion, stir to coat with the oil, and cook until browned, about 15 minutes, stirring occasionally. Put the onion in a bowl and set aside.

Using clean hands, flatten the burger patties so they are the same oval shape as the bread slices. Using your thumb, press a shallow dimple in the center of each patty so the patty cooks more evenly. Season the patties with salt and pepper. Heat the skillet over medium-high heat. Add the patties and cook until medium, about 3 minutes per side. Place the burgers on a plate and allow to rest for 2 minutes. Wipe the skillet clean with a paper towel.

Spread the dressing on the 8 slices of bread. Place 2 slices of cheese on top of each piece of bread. Add a patty and the caramelized onions to 4 pieces of bread. Top with the remaining slices of bread and their cheese slices.

Melt 1 tablespoon butter in the skillet over medium heat. Place 2 sandwiches in the skillet, cover, and cook until the bread is golden brown, about 3 minutes. Add another tablespoon of butter to the pan, turn the sandwiches over, cover, and continue to cook until golden brown and the cheese is melted. Repeat to cook the remaining 2 sandwiches. Slice the sandwiches diagonally before serving.

 **SUPERMARKET**SHORTCUT

Thousand Island dressing

Onions

Since diced, sliced, chopped, and minced onions play such important roles in my recipes, what kind to buy and how to cook them to bring out their inherent sweetness bears repeating in *Comfort Food Shortcuts*. For example, cooked onions are piled on Oooey-Gooey Patty Melts (page 83). And you're one step closer to getting Panade (page 200) on the table if you have a stash of caramelized onions in the fridge or freezer.

How long it takes to cook onions until soft, translucent, or caramelized all depends on the kind of fat used (butter, oil, or bacon drippings), the size of the skillet (the wider the better so there's more surface area), the level of heat (the lower the better), and how thinly or thickly the onions are sliced. Unless otherwise specified, I use yellow, also called Spanish, onions. If you're short on time, you can purchase sliced, diced, and chopped fresh onions as well as frozen ones.

Since making caramelized onions takes a good 30 minutes (about 15 minutes if thinly sliced) over low and slow heat, I make a big batch using 6 onions in my biggest skillet. Once cooked and cooled, the onions can be refrigerated (for up to 5 days) or frozen (for 1 month) for future use. When slicing or dicing onions, make sure the pieces are the same size for even cooking.

SOFT ONIONS: Cook the onions in a skillet, stirring frequently, with some fat over low heat for 4 to 5 minutes.

———

TRANSLUCENT ONIONS: Cook the onions in a skillet with some fat over low heat, stirring frequently, for 5 to 6 minutes, until they turn pale white.

———

CARAMELIZED ONIONS: Cook the onions in a skillet with some fat over low heat. Toss the onions to coat them with the fat. As the onions cook, they will release a lot of water that will quickly evaporate. Cook the onions, stirring frequently, until they are soft and browned, 30 to 40 minutes. If the onions start to burn, add a little water and lower the heat.

Salisbury Steak

When I was growing up, whenever my family went out to dinner, I'd order the elegant-sounding Salisbury steak, because my mom didn't make it at home. Although it's made with ground meat, Salisbury steak has more of a meatloaf-like consistency and is served with onions, mushrooms, and brown gravy. You can make this in no time by using a few shortcuts—like a pouch of onion soup mix for seasoning and a jar of beef gravy for the finish. I've always loved this dish with steamed broccoli. You may also serve it with buttered noodles or mashed potatoes.

MAKES 4 SERVINGS

1 pound lean ground beef

⅓ cup plain dry bread crumbs

1 1.4-ounce pouch onion soup mix

1 large egg, lightly beaten

1 teaspoon vegetable oil

1 12-ounce jar brown gravy

1 large yellow onion, halved and thinly sliced

5 large white mushrooms, quartered

1 tablespoon minced fresh thyme leaves

½ teaspoon freshly ground black pepper

Combine the beef, bread crumbs, onion soup mix, and egg. Using clean hands, combine the ingredients well. Divide the mixture into 4 oval patties about 1 inch thick.

Heat the oil in a large skillet over medium-high heat. Add the patties and cook until browned on both sides, about 1 minute per side. Add the gravy, onion, mushrooms, thyme, and pepper. Cover the skillet, then reduce the heat to medium-low and cook until the patties are cooked through, 15 to 17 minutes. Serve the hot patties with the gravy.

 SUPERMARKETSHORTCUTS

onion soup mix • brown gravy

Beef Tenderloin with Tarragon Sauce

Beef tenderloin is one of the most elegant and easiest meats to prepare. Be sure to season the meat well. Tenderloin cooks quickly, so it is absolutely essential to use a meat thermometer. Tarragon gives the sauce its distinctive flavor. On the side, include roasted asparagus, cheesy scalloped potatoes, and a green salad.

MAKES 6 SERVINGS

1 cup (8 ounces) mayonnaise
¼ cup packed chopped fresh
   tarragon leaves
2 tablespoons fresh lemon juice
1 tablespoon white vinegar
½ teaspoon ground turmeric
½ teaspoon plus 1 tablespoon
   freshly ground black pepper

¼ teaspoon plus 1 tablespoon
   kosher salt
1 tablespoon plus 1 tablespoon
   vegetable oil
1 2½-to-3-pound trimmed beef
   tenderloin roast

Heat the oven to 425°F. Line a sheet pan with aluminum foil. Place a wire rack in the pan.

Whisk together the mayonnaise, tarragon, lemon juice, vinegar, turmeric, the ½ teaspoon pepper, and the ¼ teaspoon salt in a bowl. Set the sauce aside.

Rub 1 tablespoon oil all over the meat, then season it with the remaining 1 tablespoon pepper and 1 tablespoon salt. Heat the remaining 1 tablespoon oil in a large skillet over high heat. Sear the meat on all sides until browned, about 5 minutes. Transfer the meat to the prepared sheet pan. Roast until an instant-read thermometer inserted into the thickest part registers 130°F for medium-rare, about 35 to 40 minutes. Remove from the oven and allow it to rest for 10 minutes.

Transfer the tenderloin to a cutting board and slice into ½-inch-thick slices. Serve with the tarragon sauce.

Mexican Tortilla Stack

Each tortilla layer is spread with refried beans, taco sauce, cheese, salsa, onions and peppers, and ground meat. Once baked, slice it into wedges.

MAKES 4 SERVINGS

1 teaspoon vegetable oil
1 pound lean ground beef
1 cup frozen chopped peppers and onions
1 8-ounce bottle taco sauce
3 8-inch flour tortillas

1 16-ounce can refried beans
1½ cups (12 ounces) shredded extra-sharp Cheddar
¼ cup pitted and sliced black olives
¼ cup chopped scallions
¼ cup (2 ounces) sour cream

Heat the oven to 375°F. Line a sheet pan with aluminum foil.

Heat the oil in a skillet over medium-high heat. Add the ground beef and the peppers and onions. Cook, stirring occasionally to brown and break the beef up into small pieces, about 7 minutes. Tilt the skillet and, using a spoon, discard any excess fat. Stir in the taco sauce to combine. Turn off the heat.

Put the tortillas in a single layer on the prepared sheet pan and bake until slightly crisp, about 10 minutes. Remove the sheet pan from the oven but keep the heat on. Spread ⅓ of the refried beans on top of a tortilla, followed by ⅓ of the beef mixture and ½ cup of Cheddar. Repeat the process with the remaining tortillas, beans, beef, and Cheddar. Bake until heated through, about 25 minutes.

Slide the stack onto a cutting board and let sit for 5 minutes before slicing into 4 wedges. Garnish with the black olives, scallions, and sour cream.

SUPERMARKETSHORTCUTS

taco sauce • refried beans

Bacon-Wrapped Meatloaf

This classic is made even better with the addition of some divine swine. Fold some chopped bacon into the meat mixture. How divine. Equal parts beef, pork, and veal are packaged together and sold as meatloaf mix in supermarkets.

MAKES 8 SERVINGS

1 pound sliced bacon
2½ pounds meatloaf mix
1 cup minced yellow onions
⅔ cup seasoned Italian bread crumbs
½ cup milk
2 large eggs, lightly beaten

3 tablespoons Worcestershire sauce
2¼ teaspoons freshly ground black pepper
1¾ teaspoons garlic salt
½ cup ketchup

Heat the oven to 350°F.

Set aside 9 slices of bacon. Chop the remaining bacon.

Place the chopped bacon, meatloaf mix, onions, bread crumbs, milk, eggs, Worcestershire sauce, pepper, and garlic salt in a bowl. Using clean hands, combine the meatloaf mixture, but don't overmix.

Place the mixture in a 9 x 13-inch baking pan and shape into a loaf form. Arrange the reserved 9 bacon slices over the loaf, overlapping them slightly and tucking underneath to keep them from curling while the meatloaf cooks. Bake the meatloaf for 1½ hours, until an instant-read thermometer inserted in the center registers 160°F. Turn the broiler to high and broil the meatloaf until the bacon is browned and crisp, about 3 minutes.

Remove the meatloaf from the oven and brush the ketchup on top. Let the meatloaf rest for 5 minutes, then remove to a cutting board and slice.

SUPERMARKETSHORTCUT

meatloaf mix

Chicken

WHETHER IT'S FRIED, ROASTED, BARBECUED, GRILLED, BROILED, OR SAUTÉED, Americans eat about ninety pounds of chicken per person every year. That's twice the amount of other meats. It makes sense, since chicken is so readily available, economical, and sold either whole or cut up so you can choose your favorite parts. The challenge is to climb out of the rut of making the same-old-same-old recipes.

Here you'll find reinvented classics that take advantage of supermarket shortcuts. Chicken Parmesan Casserole uses frozen precooked breaded chicken cutlets, so you don't have to spend time dredging and frying. Often, Indian recipes call for as many as fifteen spices, but all you need for my Chicken Tikka Masala is one spice blend such as garam masala and some red curry paste from a jar. For Bang Bang Chicken, boneless chicken breast cubes are quickly fried and then drizzled with a dressing of mayonnaise, sweet chili sauce, and hot sauce.

Think of a store-bought rotisserie chicken as your new best time-saving friend. It's amazing how many dishes—such as Chicken Carbonara and Chicken Potpie with Biscuit Topping—can be made from one already-cooked chicken.

With these recipes, you'll always hear, "Winner, winner, chicken dinner!"

Weeknight Roasted Ranch Chicken

Once a week, my mom roasted a whole chicken which doesn't take long to cook. The ranch seasoning provides all the flavoring you need.

MAKES 6 SERVINGS

1 4-to-5-pound chicken

5 tablespoons salted butter, melted

2 tablespoons minced fresh thyme leaves

1 1-ounce packet dry ranch salad dressing mix

3 garlic cloves, minced

1 cup (8 ounces) each equal amounts celery, onions, and carrots, cut into 2-inch pieces

Heat the oven to 400°F. Rinse the chicken and its cavity with cold water, then pat dry all over with paper towels.

Combine the butter, thyme, ranch mix, and garlic in a bowl. Using your fingers, gently separate the skin from the breast meat and, trying not to tear the skin, insert half of the ranch mixture under the skin. Rub the remaining ranch mixture all over the outside of the chicken.

Place the chicken, breast side up, in a roasting pan. Arrange the celery, onions, and carrots around the chicken.

Roast the chicken until an instant-read thermometer inserted into the thickest part of the thigh but not touching the bone registers 165°F, about 1 hour. Remove from the oven and let rest for 10 minutes before carving and serving with the vegetables and pan juices.

 **SUPERMARKET**SHORTCUT

dry ranch salad dressing mix

Creamy French Onion Chicken Casserole

Except for grating the sharp Cheddar and grinding the black pepper, every ingredient in this casserole is a supermarket shortcut! The whole dish can be baked ahead and reheated, except for the canned French-fried onions, which are scattered on top just before serving.

MAKES 8 SERVINGS

1 rotisserie chicken, meat removed and shredded

2 8.8-ounce packages Uncle Ben's® Ready Rice®

2 cups frozen peas and carrots

2 cups shredded extra-sharp Cheddar

1 10½-ounce can condensed cream of chicken soup

1 2-ounce package onion soup mix

1¾ teaspoons freshly ground black pepper

1 6-ounce can French-fried onions

Heat the oven to 350°F.

Put the chicken meat, rice, 2½ cups water, the peas and carrots, Cheddar, chicken soup, onion soup mix, and pepper in a bowl. Stir well to combine. Pour the mixture into a 9 x 13-inch baking pan. Bake until heated through, 50 to 55 minutes. Evenly sprinkle the fried onions on the top before serving.

 SUPERMARKETSHORTCUTS

rotisserie chicken • Uncle Ben's® Ready Rice • frozen peas and carrots • condensed cream of chicken soup • onion soup mix • French-fried onions

Chicken Parmesan Casserole

Yes, you can make chicken Parm on a weeknight! Everything we love about this classic dish is here, but without the time-consuming hassle. Instead of pounding and frying chicken breasts, frozen breaded chicken cutlets are used along with your favorite jarred sauce. Round out the meal with a crisp Caesar salad, some toasty garlic bread, and your favorite red wine.

MAKES 8 TO 10 SERVINGS

2 tablespoons kosher salt

3 cups (8 to 10 ounces) penne

2 pounds frozen breaded chicken cutlets, thawed and cut into 1-inch pieces

2 24-ounce jars tomato-and-basil pasta sauce

¾ cup (3 ounces) grated Parmigiano-Reggiano

1½ cups (12 ounces) shredded Italian Fontina

1½ cups (12 ounces) shredded mozzarella

½ cup chopped fresh basil

Heat the oven to 350°F.

Bring a large pot of water to a boil and add the salt. Add the penne and cook, stirring occasionally, until tender but still firm to the bite. Drain the penne in a colander and put in a mixing bowl. Add the chicken pieces, pasta sauce, Parmigiano-Reggiano, and Fontina and stir well to combine. Pour the mixture into a 9 x 13-inch baking dish. Cover with aluminum foil and bake for 35 minutes. Remove the foil and sprinkle the mozzarella evenly on top. Bake until heated through and the cheeses are melted, about 25 minutes. Let sit for 5 to 10 minutes, then sprinkle with the basil before serving.

 SUPERMARKETSHORTCUTS

frozen breaded chicken cutlets • shredded mozzarella

Chicken Potpie with Biscuit Topping

Chicken potpie is a classic, but it does take time to make when you start from scratch. My version uses cooked meat from a rotisserie chicken mixed with frozen vegetables and cream of chicken soup. The casserole is topped with refrigerator biscuits and then baked. To save even more time, warm the filling first in a stockpot and then pour it into a casserole. Then it needs just thirty minutes in the oven.

MAKES 6 SERVINGS

1 rotisserie chicken, meat removed and shredded

1 16-ounce bag frozen mixed vegetables

2 10½-ounce cans condensed cream of chicken soup

2 cups low-sodium chicken broth

1 teaspoon freshly ground black pepper

1 16.3-ounce can Grands!™ Flaky Layers Buttermilk Biscuits

Heat the oven to 350°F.

Put the chicken, vegetables, cream of chicken soup, broth, and pepper in a large pot. Bring the mixture to a boil, stirring occasionally, and then pour into a 9 x 13-inch baking pan. Arrange the biscuits evenly on top of the chicken mixture. Bake until the biscuits are golden brown and cooked through, about 30 minutes.

SUPERMARKETSHORTCUTS

rotisserie chicken • frozen mixed vegetables • condensed cream of chicken soup • low-sodium chicken broth • Grands!™ Flaky Layers Buttermilk Biscuits

Chicken Cacciatore

Cacciatore means "hunter style" in Italian. The chicken is braised on the stove top in a tomato-based sauce. It's traditional to serve chicken cacciatore over rice, but mashed potatoes or noodles work, too. I also suggest a loaf of crusty bread to sop up more of the savory sauce.

MAKES 4 SERVINGS

2 pounds bone-in, skin-on chicken thighs

1 teaspoon kosher salt

1 teaspoon freshly ground black pepper

1 cup thinly sliced yellow onions

1 red bell pepper, seeded and thinly sliced

6 garlic cloves, thinly sliced

1 28-ounce can diced tomatoes, drained

½ cup pimiento-stuffed green olives

1 teaspoon Italian seasoning

½ cup shredded fresh basil

Season the chicken thighs with the salt and pepper.

Heat a large skillet over medium-high heat. Add the chicken, skin side down, to the skillet and cook until browned, about 5 minutes. Remove the chicken to a plate and set aside. Leave any drippings in the skillet.

Add the onions, bell pepper, and garlic to the same skillet. Reduce the heat to medium and cook, stirring occasionally, until the onions are translucent, 5 to 6 minutes. Stir in the tomatoes, olives, and Italian seasoning.

Return the chicken to the skillet with the sauce, skin side up. Reduce the heat to medium-low, cover, and cook until the chicken is cooked through, about 30 minutes. Stir in the basil and serve.

 **SUPERMARKET**SHORTCUTS

pimiento-stuffed green olives • Italian seasoning

Chicken Carbonara

Spaghetti carbonara traditionally includes eggs in the sauce, but there's always a risk of undercooking them or overcooking them so they scramble. In place of eggs, I use mascarpone (look for it near the cream cheese) to make a creamy sauce that holds together. Cut the meat off a rotisserie chicken for easy preparation. Cook the spaghetti in a large pot and drain it. Quickly put the sauce together in the same pot that the spaghetti was cooked in, then combine everything for a surprisingly easy and delicious meal.

MAKES 6 TO 8 SERVINGS

1 tablespoon plus ½ teaspoon kosher salt

1 pound spaghetti

1 tablespoon olive oil

8 ounces smoked cured turkey bacon, chopped

1 rotisserie chicken, meat removed and shredded

1¾ cups low-sodium chicken broth

2 8-ounce containers mascarpone

¾ cup frozen peas

3 garlic cloves, minced

1 teaspoon freshly ground black pepper

Bring a large pot of water and the 1 tablespoon salt to a boil. Add the spaghetti and, stirring occasionally, cook until tender but still firm to the bite. Drain the spaghetti in a colander, but do not rinse it.

Heat the oil in the same pot over medium-high heat. Add the turkey bacon and cook until browned, about 5 minutes. Stir in the chicken, broth, mascarpone, peas, garlic, the remaining ½ teaspoon salt, the pepper, and the drained spaghetti. Reduce the heat to medium and cook, stirring frequently, about 10 minutes, until everything is well combined. Divide among bowls and serve.

 SUPERMARKETSHORTCUTS

turkey bacon • rotisserie chicken • low-sodium chicken broth • mascarpone • frozen peas

Chicken Tikka Masala

I've been eager to learn more about Indian food, especially having tried this easy dish. Chicken breasts are marinated for at least 6 hours or overnight in a blend of yogurt and an Indian spice mix called garam masala, then baked. While some people prefer to make their own spice blend, buying premixed garam masala saves time because all the fragrant spices—cumin, turmeric, black pepper, cardamom, cloves, coriander, and nutmeg—are already combined. Look for garam masala in the spice aisle. Serve the chicken with white rice, a side of sautéed spinach, and some warm Indian bread such as naan.

MAKES 6 SERVINGS

½ cup nonfat plain Greek yogurt
3 tablespoons fresh lemon juice
2 tablespoons Thai red curry paste
1 tablespoon garam masala
1 teaspoon kosher salt
1 teaspoon freshly ground black pepper

2½ pounds boneless, skinless chicken breasts, cut into 1½- to 2-inch chunks
1 tablespoon vegetable oil
1 8-ounce can tomato sauce
¼ cup chopped fresh cilantro

In a large bowl, combine the yogurt, lemon juice, curry paste, garam masala, salt, and pepper and mix well with a rubber spatula. Fold in the chicken and toss to coat with the yogurt mixture. Cover and refrigerate the chicken mixture for 6 hours or overnight.

Heat the oil in a large skillet over medium-high heat. Add the chicken in a single layer and cook, stirring occasionally, until lightly browned, 5 to 6 minutes. Stir in the tomato sauce, then reduce the heat to medium-low. Cover and cook until the chicken is tender and cooked through, about 10 minutes. Garnish with the cilantro.

 **SUPERMARKET**SHORTCUTS
Thai red curry paste • garam masala

Bang Bang Chicken

Bang Bang Chicken got its name from the sound made when chicken breasts were pounded to make them tender. Thank goodness, we can now purchase tender boneless, skinless chicken breasts that just need to be cut into pieces before they're cooked. The nuggets are drizzled with a sweet chili mayonnaise that can be made ahead of time.

MAKES 6 TO 8 SERVINGS

1 cup (8 ounces) mayonnaise

1 6.4-ounce bottle sweet chili sauce

¼ cup hot sauce

1¼ cups half-and-half

½ cup all-purpose flour

⅓ cup cornstarch

1 large egg

1 teaspoon plus ½ teaspoon kosher salt

2½ cups panko (Japanese bread crumbs)

Vegetable oil for frying

2 pounds boneless, skinless chicken breasts, cut into 1- to 1½-inch pieces

Whisk together the mayonnaise, chili sauce, and hot sauce in a bowl. Set aside.

Whisk together the half-and-half, flour, cornstarch, egg, and the 1 teaspoon salt in a shallow bowl. Combine the panko and the remaining ½ teaspoon salt in a second shallow bowl.

Add ¼ inch oil to a large skillet and heat over medium heat. Dip the chicken pieces into the half-and-half mixture, then, 1 at a time, dip each chicken piece into the panko, pressing gently to coat.

Working in batches to avoid overcrowding the skillet, add some of the chicken pieces and fry until golden brown on all sides and cooked through, 4 to 5 minutes. Put the cooked chicken on paper towels to drain while cooking the rest. Serve hot, drizzled with the sauce.

SUPERMARKETSHORTCUTS

sweet chili sauce • panko

Barbecued Chicken Thighs

Bone-in chicken thighs are the meatiest and juiciest parts of the bird. Here, they are marinated in a combination of hoisin, ketchup, and soy sauce with a bit of spicy Sriracha. Once baked until tender, you can add another level of texture to the thighs by broiling them for three or four minutes until the skin is dark and crisp.

MAKES 6 TO 8 SERVINGS

1 cup hoisin sauce
¾ cup ketchup
¼ cup soy sauce
6 garlic cloves, minced
2 tablespoons Sriracha
2 tablespoons minced fresh ginger

1½ teaspoons freshly ground black pepper
6 pounds skin-on, bone-in chicken thighs, trimmed of any fat
1 teaspoon sesame seeds
¼ cup thinly sliced scallions

Whisk together the hoisin sauce, ketchup, soy sauce, garlic, Sriracha, ginger, and pepper in a bowl. Put the chicken thighs in a zip-closed plastic bag, add the marinade, seal, and toss to coat. Put the bag in a dish to catch any leaks and refrigerate the chicken for 8 hours or overnight.

Heat the oven to 425°F. Line a sheet pan with aluminum foil.

Arrange the marinated chicken, skin side up, on a sheet pan in a single layer. Bake until an instant-read thermometer inserted into the chicken thighs registers 165°F, 30 to 35 minutes. Sprinkle on the sesame seeds and scallions before serving.

SUPERMARKETSHORTCUTS

hoisin sauce • Sriracha

Chicken Milanese

Thin chicken cutlets are dredged in a seasoned crumb coating and panfried, then topped with peppery arugula and cherry tomatoes and garnished with lemon wedges for squeezing over the entire dish.

MAKES 4 SERVINGS

4 (4 to 6 ounces each) boneless, skinless chicken breasts

1 teaspoon plus ½ teaspoon kosher salt

1 teaspoon plus ½ teaspoon freshly ground black pepper

¼ cup all-purpose flour

1 large egg

1 cup seasoned Italian bread crumbs

¼ cup (1 ounce) grated Parmigiano-Reggiano

1 teaspoon garlic powder

Vegetable oil for frying

4 cups arugula

1 cup cherry tomatoes, halved

Lemon wedges

Put 1 chicken breast on a piece of plastic wrap and cover with another piece of plastic wrap. Using a rolling pin, pound the chicken breast to a thickness of ¼ inch. Repeat with the remaining chicken breasts. Remove the plastic wrap and season the chicken with the 1 teaspoon salt and the 1 teaspoon pepper.

Put the flour in a shallow bowl. Put the egg in another shallow bowl and beat with 2 tablespoons water. Put the bread crumbs, Parmegiano-Reggiano, garlic powder, and the remaining ½ teaspoon salt and ½ teaspoon pepper in a third shallow bowl and mix well. Dip each chicken breast into the flour, coating evenly on both sides, then the egg mixture, followed by the bread crumbs, shaking off any excess mixture and pressing firmly to coat.

Add ¼ inch oil to a large skillet and heat over medium heat. Cook the chicken until golden brown, 2 to 2½ minutes per side. Put the chicken on a paper towel–lined plate to absorb any excess oil. Serve with arugula and cherry tomatoes, with the lemon wedges alongside.

Pork

PORK. JUST THE MERE MENTION OF THE WORD MAKES MY TASTE BUDS TINGLE, my mouth water, and my lips smack in happy-dance anticipation. Ever since I was little and learning how to cook from my mom, pork has always been among my favorite meats, which is why I call it "the divine swine."

From ribs to tenderloins, from cutlets to chops, these and other parts of the pig can be panfried, slow-cooked, stir-fried, roasted, grilled, pressure-cooked, barbecued, and so much more. Succulent, meaty, and juicy pork can have a crisp crust while being falling-off-the-bone tender at the same time. Boneless country ribs flavored with fajita seasoning can be pressure-cooked in less than an hour. Dress up bone-in pork chops by filling them with some seasoned stuffing mix and spinach, then sear and oven-bake them. A lean pork tenderloin with a quick mustard-cream pan sauce is perfect for a weeknight or weekend celebration.

Oh, did I mention bacon, the best part of the pig? Don't get me started.

Barbecued Pulled Pork Casserole

This dish has everything I love in one convenient casserole. Precooked and shredded pulled pork, a can of baked beans, and some barbecue sauce are combined in a skillet, then I top it with a yummy cornbread batter and bake it. The result is a barbecued shepherd's pie, ideal for a weeknight meal or a summer dinner on the picnic table. Coleslaw or potato salad are my go-to sides with this dish.

MAKES 6 SERVINGS

1 8.5-ounce box Jiffy Corn Muffin Mix

1 cup (4 ounces) shredded extra-sharp Cheddar

1 large egg

½ cup buttermilk

1 1½-pound package precooked pulled pork

1 16-ounce can baked beans

1½ cups bottled barbecue sauce

1 red bell pepper, seeded and chopped

1 green bell pepper, seeded and chopped

Heat the oven to 350°F.

Whisk together the corn muffin mix, Cheddar, egg, and buttermilk in a bowl.

Put the pulled pork, baked beans, barbecue sauce, and red and green bell peppers in an ovenproof skillet over medium-high heat. Cook, stirring occasionally, until heated through, 6 to 7 minutes. Evenly spread the cornbread mixture over the pork mixture, smoothing the top and sealing the edges. Bake until a toothpick inserted into just the corn bread comes out clean, about 35 minutes. Remove from the oven and let rest for 10 minutes prior to serving.

 SUPERMARKETSHORTCUTS

corn muffin mix • precooked pulled pork • baked beans • barbecue sauce

Roasted Pork Tenderloin with Mustard Cream

This dish is so fancy, it's hard to believe that it's so easy to prepare. The steak seasoning makes these tenderloins mouthwatering, and the velvety mustard cream is the perfect finishing touch.

MAKES 6 TO 8 SERVINGS

1 cup heavy cream
½ cup chopped yellow onion
¼ cup Dijon mustard
1 tablespoon minced fresh
   rosemary leaves

1 tablespoon plus ½ tablespoon
   plus ½ tablespoon vegetable oil
2 1-pound pork tenderloins, silver
   skin removed
3 tablespoons Montreal Steak
   Seasoning

Heat the oven to 425°F. Place a wire rack on an aluminum foil–lined sheet pan.

Put the cream, onion, mustard, and rosemary in a saucepan. Bring the mixture to a boil, then reduce the heat to medium-low. Cook, stirring occasionally, until the mixture has reduced and thickened slightly, 15 to 20 minutes.

Heat the 1 tablespoon oil in a large ovenproof skillet over high heat. Rub each tenderloin with each remaining ½ tablespoon oil, then sprinkle each with 1½ tablespoons of the steak seasoning. Sear the tenderloins on all sides until browned, about 5 minutes. Transfer the tenderloins to the prepared sheet pan.

Bake until an instant-read thermometer inserted into the thickest part of the tenderloins registers 145°F, 20 to 25 minutes. Remove from the oven and let rest for 5 minutes before slicing. Serve with the warm mustard-cream sauce.

 **SUPERMARKET**SHORTCUTS

Dijon mustard • Montreal Steak Seasoning

Stuffed Pork Chops

What's better than a pork chop? A pork chop filled with spinach, cheese, and bread!

MAKES 4 SERVINGS

⅓ cup low-sodium chicken broth

2 tablespoons salted butter

1 cup seasoned stuffing cubes

½ cup frozen spinach, thawed and squeezed dry

3 tablespoons chopped fresh sage leaves

¼ teaspoon plus ¾ teaspoon kosher salt

¼ teaspoon plus ¾ teaspoon freshly ground black pepper

4 8-ounce boneless pork loin chops

¾ cup Italian Fontina, cut into ¼-inch dice

1 tablespoon vegetable oil

Heat the oven to 375°F. Line a sheet pan with aluminum foil.

Heat the broth and butter in a saucepan to melt the butter. Bring to a boil, then stir in the stuffing cubes to coat. Remove the saucepan from the heat, fluff the stuffing with a fork, and let cool. Stir the spinach, sage, the ¼ teaspoon salt, and the ¼ teaspoon pepper into the stuffing.

Cut a small pocket into each chop by slicing a 1-inch horizontal cut ¾ of the way through the meat. Put equal amounts of the Fontina, then the stuffing mixture, into the pocket of each chop. Season the chops with the remaining salt and pepper.

Heat the oil in a skillet over medium-high heat. Put the chops in the skillet and sear until browned on both sides, 2 to 3 minutes per side. Place the chops on the sheet pan. Bake the chops until cooked through, 25 to 30 minutes, or until the internal temperature reaches 165°F. Let rest for 3 minutes prior to serving.

 SUPERMARKETSHORTCUTS

low-sodium chicken broth • stuffing cubes • frozen spinach

Slow Cooker Pork Chops with Cherry Preserves and Apples

How can you possibly improve on a pairing like pork and apples? By stirring in some cherry preserves with the other ingredients when they go into the slow cooker. When you lift the lid some hours later, the pork chops will be tender and the tangy sauce will be the consistency of applesauce.

MAKES 4 SERVINGS

1 tablespoon vegetable oil

4 1¼-inch-thick boneless pork loin chops, about 2 pounds

1 teaspoon kosher salt

1 teaspoon plus ½ teaspoon freshly ground black pepper

⅔ cup cherry preserves

⅓ cup low-sodium chicken broth

1 .87-ounce packet pork gravy mix

1 tablespoon minced fresh rosemary leaves

3 apples, peeled, seeded, and cut into quarters

Heat the oil in a large skillet over medium-high heat. Season the pork with the salt and the 1 teaspoon pepper. Cook the pork on both sides until golden brown, about 2 minutes per side. Put the pork chops into the slow cooker.

Whisk together the cherry preserves, broth, gravy mix, rosemary, and the ½ teaspoon pepper. Add the cherry mixture, then the apples to the slow cooker. Cover and cook on low heat for 4 hours.

Divide the pork among four plates and ladle the sauce on top to serve.

 SUPERMARKETSHORTCUTS

cherry preserves • low-sodium chicken broth • pork gravy mix

Tex-Mex Country Ribs Under Pressure

Meaty, boneless country-style ribs cook faster than those with bones, so these are done in no time. Once seared, the ribs and fajita seasoning are put into the pressure cooker. If you like yours with some heat, stir in a bit of red pepper flakes, Sriracha, or chipotle peppers in adobo. Serve the ribs with rice and maybe some beans or shred the meat to fill tacos.

MAKES 6 TO 8 SERVINGS

1 teaspoon vegetable oil
4 to 5 pounds boneless pork
   country ribs
2 teaspoons kosher salt
1 teaspoon freshly ground black
   pepper

1 1.12-ounce package fajita
   seasoning
2 teaspoons ground cumin
4 garlic cloves, minced
½ cup chopped fresh cilantro
   leaves
Lime wedges, for serving

Heat the oil in a large skillet over medium-high heat. Season the ribs with the salt and pepper. Working in batches, add the ribs to the skillet and sear on all sides until golden brown, about 3 minutes per side.

Put the ribs, fajita seasoning, cumin, and garlic in the pressure cooker. Stir to combine. Close the lid and set the pressure to high for 50 minutes. Do a quick release. Open the lid. Serve the ribs on a platter with the sauce. Sprinkle on the cilantro and serve with the lime wedges.

SUPERMARKETSHORTCUT

fajita seasoning

Pork Stir-Fry with Cauliflower Rice

This dish includes riced low-carb cauliflower, which is readily available, so you don't have to make a separate pot of rice. For this dish, pork tenderloins are cut into pieces, then marinated for 8 hours or overnight in bottled stir-fry sauce.

MAKES 6 SERVINGS

2 1-pound pork tenderloins, silver skin removed

1 12.1-ounce bottle stir-fry sauce

2 tablespoons toasted sesame oil

1 16-ounce bag frozen Asian stir-fry vegetables

1 10-ounce bag frozen cauliflower rice

⅓ cup low-sodium chicken broth

1 tablespoon minced fresh ginger

¼ cup soy sauce

Pat the pork dry with a paper towel. Cut each tenderloin in half lengthwise, then cut crosswise into ¼-inch pieces. Put the pork in a large resealable plastic bag. Add the stir-fry sauce to the bag, seal, and toss to coat. Put the bag in a bowl and refrigerate for 8 hours or overnight.

Remove the pork from the marinade. Discard the marinade.

Heat the oil in a Dutch oven over high heat. Add the pork and cook, stirring occasionally, for 4 to 5 minutes. Put the cooked pork on a plate and leave any juices in the pot.

Add the stir-fry vegetables, cauliflower rice, broth, and ginger to the pot. Cover and cook, stirring occasionally, until the vegetables are tender, about 8 minutes. Add the cooked pork and soy sauce to the pot. Stir to combine and serve.

 SUPERMARKETSHORTCUTS

stir-fry sauce • frozen Asian stir-fry vegetables • cauliflower rice • low-sodium chicken broth

Cauliflower Rice

If you find yourself with a head or two of cauliflower, it's easy to make your own cauliflower rice. Pull a head of cauliflower apart into 1- to 2-inch florets. Put the cauliflower in a food processor and pulse two or three times until the mixture looks like rice. If the cauliflower is large, you may have to do this in batches. You can freeze uncooked cauliflower rice for up to 1 month. When ready to use, choose from one of these methods.

To cook on the stove top: Heat 1 or 2 tablespoons of cooking oil in a skillet over medium-high heat. Add the cauliflower rice and cook, stirring occasionally, until brown, about 8 minutes. Season with salt and pepper and herbs and spices of your choosing.

To cook in the oven: Heat the oven to 400°F. Line a sheet pan with parchment paper. Put the rice in a bowl, drizzle on some oil, then season with salt and pepper, and toss to coat. Evenly spread the rice on the sheet pan and bake, stirring 2 or 3 times, until lightly browned, 20 to 25 minutes.

Panfried Pork Schnitzel with Lemon Cream

During my early days at QVC, when I was sent to Germany to purchase collectibles, my colleagues and I traveled from quaint village to quaint village looking for wares made by small producers. Whether we stopped for something to eat on the bustling Autobahn or along two-lane back-country roads, every restaurant offered *schweinefleisch* (pork) or *weiner* schnitzel (veal). The cutlets were thinly pounded and quickly panfried and served with a mountain-sized portion of *pommes frites* (French fries). Being the divine-swine fan that I am, I seized the opportunity to try as much pork schnitzel as I could.

MAKES 4 SERVINGS

Sauce

½ cup (4 ounces) sour cream
2 tablespoons fresh lemon juice
1 teaspoon dried dill
¼ teaspoon kosher salt
¼ teaspoon freshly ground black pepper

Schnitzel

4 6-ounce boneless pork loin chops
½ teaspoon plus ¾ teaspoon kosher salt
½ teaspoon plus ½ teaspoon freshly ground black pepper
¼ cup all-purpose flour
1 large egg
¾ cup plain dry bread crumbs
Vegetable oil for frying

To make the sauce, whisk together the sour cream, lemon juice, dill, ¼ teaspoon salt, and ¼ teaspoon pepper in a bowl. Set aside. The sauce can be made ahead and refrigerated.

To make the schnitzel, place a pork chop between two pieces of plastic wrap. Using the flat side of a mallet or a rolling pin, pound the pork chop to a ¼-inch thickness. Remove from the plastic and set aside. Repeat with the remaining chops. Season the pork chops with the ½ teaspoon salt and ½ teaspoon pepper.

Put the flour in a shallow bowl. Beat the egg and 2 tablespoons water in another shallow bowl. Combine the bread crumbs, the ¾ teaspoon salt, and the remaining ½ teaspoon pepper in a third shallow bowl.

Add ¼ inch oil to a large, deep skillet and heat over medium heat.

One at a time, dip the chops evenly into the flour, then the egg mixture, followed by the bread crumbs, shaking off any excess mixture and pressing firmly to coat.

Working in batches, add the breaded chops to the skillet and cook until golden brown, 2 to 3 minutes on each side. Place the chops onto a paper towel–lined plate to absorb any excess oil. Serve the schnitzel with the sauce.

Grilled Coiled Sausage

When I was in college, I went to Switzerland on an exchange program with some other students. One of the host families invited everyone to a backyard barbecue. I'll never forget the huge, coiled smoky sausage and vegetables that they put on the grill. But what impressed me most was the tangy mustard that came in a tube, like toothpaste, rather than a jar!

MAKES 6 SERVINGS

1 red bell pepper, seeded and cut into quarters

1 green bell pepper, seeded and cut into quarters

1 red onion, cut into ½-inch rounds

1 medium yellow squash, cut into ½-inch rounds

⅓ cup Italian vinaigrette

2 12-inch-long skewers (soak wooden skewers in water for 20 minutes)

1 3-pound Italian sausage coil

Whole-grain or Dijon mustard, for serving

Heat the grill to medium-high heat.

Put the red and green peppers, onion, and yellow squash in a bowl. Add the Italian vinaigrette and toss the vegetables to coat.

Insert 2 skewers through the sausage coil, forming an X shape. Put the sausage and vegetables on the grill. Cook the vegetables until lightly charred and tender, turning once. Cook the sausage until golden brown on the bottom, 10 to 12 minutes, then use a large spatula to turn the sausage over and cook on the other side for 10 to 12 minutes. Remove the sausage to a cutting board and cut into large pieces. Serve with the grilled vegetables and mustard.

SUPERMARKETSHORTCUT

Italian vinaigrette

Grilled Kielbasa Tacos

Looking for a new idea for taco night? Smoky kielbasa sausages are split and sliced again, then quickly cooked in a stove-top grill pan. Be sure to marinate the onions for 8 hours or overnight. Serve with all the traditional taco accompaniments—avocado, cilantro, and lime wedges—and a side of Mexican Street Corn Off the Cob (page 196).

MAKES 4 SERVINGS

1 ½ cups thinly sliced red onions
⅔ cup white vinegar
1 teaspoon kosher salt
1 teaspoon sugar
1 14-ounce package kielbasa
2 red bell peppers, seeded and
   thinly sliced

8 6-inch flour tortillas
2 avocados, pitted, peeled, and
   sliced
1 cup fresh cilantro leaves
2 limes, cut into 8 wedges

Put the onions in a bowl. Add the vinegar, salt, and sugar to a saucepan. Bring to a boil, stir to dissolve the salt and sugar, and then pour the mixture over the onions. Cover and refrigerate for 8 hours or overnight.

Slice the kielbasa into 4 equal-sized pieces, then cut the slices into lengthwise pieces.

Heat a grill pan over medium-high heat. Working in batches, add the bell peppers and cook, tossing occasionally, until tender, about 5 minutes. Remove the peppers to a platter. Put the kielbasa pieces into the grill pan and cook until lightly charred on both sides, about 5 minutes. Add the cooked sausage to the peppers. Cover with aluminum foil to keep warm. One by one, heat the tortillas on both sides in the grill pan until warm.

For each taco, put 2 pieces of kielbasa in the middle of each tortilla. Top with the grilled peppers, avocado slices, pickled onions, and cilantro. Serve with the lime wedges on the side.

Smoked Ham and Cheddar Hash

While we usually think of hash as a breakfast or brunch dish, this hearty casserole is also ideal for the dinner table. You can use store-bought ham or repurpose any that's left over from a previous meal. The hash is started on the stove top, then finished in the oven, so it can be made ahead and baked the next day.

MAKES 6 SERVINGS

3 tablespoons salted butter

1 large yellow onion, chopped

4 cups (20 ounces) diced precooked smoked ham steak

3 cups diced frozen hash brown potatoes

1 10½-ounce can condensed cream of mushroom soup

¾ cup low-sodium chicken broth

1 teaspoon freshly ground black pepper

1 teaspoon smoked paprika

2 cups (8 ounces) shredded extra-sharp Cheddar

¾ cup panko (Japanese bread crumbs)

Heat the oven to 400°F.

Melt the butter in a large ovenproof skillet over medium-high heat. Add the onion and cook, stirring occasionally until lightly browned, about 10 minutes.

Stir in the ham, hash browns, cream of mushroom soup, broth, pepper, and smoked paprika and bring to a simmer.

Put the Cheddar and bread crumbs in a bowl and stir well to blend. Evenly sprinkle the cheese mixture on top of the hash. Bake for 20 minutes or until lightly browned on top. Let sit for 5 minutes before serving.

 SUPERMARKETSHORTCUTS

precooked ham steak • diced frozen hash browns • condensed cream of mushroom soup • low-sodium chicken broth • panko

Seafood

OF ALL THE CHOICES YOU HAVE FOR DINNER, NOTHING COOKS QUICKER THAN fresh fish and shellfish. Fresh is the key word when buying seafood. Ask the person behind the counter when the seafood was delivered to the store. That morning or the previous day is fine; any longer than that, shop elsewhere. The other tip is to cook seafood for less, rather than more, time. Always err on the side of undercooking, because you can put the flounder back in the oven or return the sea scallops to the pan for another thirty seconds. Nothing ruins good fish or shellfish like overcooking.

Summer Shrimp and Pasta Salad is done once the rotini is cooked and just needs an hour to chill. Salmon spends just ten minutes in a skillet and is accompanied by grape tomatoes and two favorite supermarket shortcuts: roasted red peppers from a jar and balsamic glaze. A huge pot of steamed mussels makes a great starter at a casual dinner party. Even better, all of my seafood recipes take less than thirty minutes to cook.

Roasted Cod

Fish fillets are arranged on individual sheets of aluminum foil, what we call "tinfoil" down South. Then the fish is spread with some pesto, surrounded by vegetables, then tightly sealed and baked to keep everything moist. Once it's baked, use a spatula to remove the fish, vegetables, and sauce to dinner plates.

MAKES 4 SERVINGS

4 6-ounce fresh cod, halibut, or striped bass fillets
½ teaspoon kosher salt
½ teaspoon freshly ground black pepper

¼ cup pesto
1¼ cups cherry tomatoes
1 red bell pepper, seeded and cut into strips
2 shallots, thinly sliced

Heat the oven to 425°F. Cut four 12-inch square sheets of aluminum foil and place on a work surface.

Place a cod fillet in the middle of each foil sheet. Season with salt and pepper.

Evenly coat the top of each fillet with 1 tablespoon pesto. Arrange the tomatoes, bell pepper, and shallots around each fillet. Wrap the foil around the fish, ensuring that the seal is tight and facing up.

Place the cod packets on a sheet pan and bake until the cod is cooked through, 23 to 25 minutes. You can place each packet on a dinner plate to serve, or use a spatula to move the fish and vegetables to the plates.

 **SUPERMARKET**SHORTCUT

pesto

Salmon Fillets with Balsamic Glaze

Salmon is a close second to shrimp as the most popular seafood in America, which makes sense because they're both so easy to cook and can be paired with so many kinds of seasonings. Think of salmon as the chicken of the sea. So versatile, salmon can be grilled, roasted, poached, or panfried, and served with all kinds of vegetables, grains, and other sides.

MAKES 4 SERVINGS

1 teaspoon vegetable oil

4 6-ounce salmon fillets

½ teaspoon kosher salt

½ teaspoon freshly ground black pepper

1½ cups grape tomatoes

1 cup jarred roasted and sliced red peppers

Balsamic glaze

¼ cup chopped fresh basil leaves

Heat the oil in a large skillet over medium heat. Season the salmon with the salt and pepper. Add the salmon to the skillet, flesh side down, and cook until each fillet has a golden-brown crust, about 6 minutes. Using a spatula, gently turn each fillet over. Add the tomatoes and roasted red peppers. Cover the skillet and cook until the salmon is cooked through, about 4 minutes, for medium. To serve, drizzle the balsamic glaze on top and sprinkle with the basil.

 SUPERMARKETSHORTCUTS

roasted and sliced red peppers • balsamic glaze

Instant Mashed Potato–Crusted Flounder with Comeback Sauce

Comeback sauce is like a combination of tartar sauce and Thousand Island dressing. Everyone in Mississippi knows it's so good, they say "Y'all will come back for more."

MAKES 4 SERVINGS

½ cup (4 ounces) mayonnaise
⅓ cup sweet chili sauce
2 tablespoons spicy brown mustard
1 teaspoon hot sauce
¼ teaspoon plus 1 teaspoon kosher salt

¼ teaspoon plus 1 teaspoon freshly ground black pepper
Vegetable oil
4 (4 to 6 ounces each) flounder, snapper, or sole fillets
2 large eggs
2½ cups instant mashed potatoes

Whisk together the mayonnaise, chili sauce, mustard, hot sauce, the ¼ teaspoon salt, and the ¼ teaspoon pepper in a bowl. Cover and refrigerate until needed.

Heat ¼ inch vegetable oil in a deep skillet over medium heat.

Season the fish fillets with the remaining 1 teaspoon salt and 1 teaspoon pepper. Put the eggs in a shallow bowl and beat with ¼ cup water. Put the instant potatoes in another shallow bowl. Dip each fillet into the egg mixture, then into the instant potatoes, shaking off any excess and pressing firmly to coat. Repeat the process a second time.

Working in batches, fry the fish in the hot oil until golden brown, 3 to 4 minutes per side. Drain the fish on a paper towel–lined plate. Continue with the remaining fish. Serve the fish hot with the sauce on the side.

 **SUPERMARKET**SHORTCUTS
sweet chili sauce • instant mashed potatoes

Fish Tacos

The Mexican state of Baja California, where fish tacos are said to have come from, lies just below the American state of California. While fresh-from-the-ocean fish was originally fried, I prefer to bake the fillets and set out bowls of traditional condiments, so everyone can make their own tacos.

MAKES 4 SERVINGS

1½ pounds snapper, mahi mahi, grouper, or flounder fillets
1 teaspoon ground cumin
½ teaspoon kosher salt
½ teaspoon freshly ground black pepper

8 5-inch soft corn tortillas
2⅔ cups (about 8 ounces) coleslaw mix
¾ cup chopped pickled jalapeños
½ cup (4 ounces) sour cream
2 limes, cut into 8 wedges

Heat the oven to 425°F. Line a sheet pan with aluminum foil.

Cut the fish fillets into pieces about 1 x 4 inches. Season with the cumin, salt, and pepper. Put the fish on the prepared sheet pan in a single layer. Bake until cooked through, about 15 minutes.

To warm the corn tortillas, stack them on a microwave-safe plate. Lightly dampen two to three paper towels with water, then cover the tortillas. Microwave for 1 minute. If still not warm, repeat in 30-second intervals. Place 1 piece of cooked fish in the middle of each tortilla and, using a fork, gently flake the fish into pieces. Top with the coleslaw mix, jalapeños, and sour cream. Serve with lime wedges on the side.

 SUPERMARKETSHORTCUTS

coleslaw mix • pickled jalapeños

Summer Shrimp and Pasta Salad

Nothing beats a shrimp and pasta salad on a warm summer night. Adding a bit of Old Bay Seasoning reminds me of summers spent on Maryland's Chesapeake Bay. Spoon the salad onto lettuce leaves and accompany with fresh-from-the-garden cherry tomatoes and perhaps some blanched green beans dressed with olive oil and lemon juice. While this recipe calls for tricolor rotini, you can substitute macaroni, fusilli, or small shells.

MAKES 6 SERVINGS

1 tablespoon kosher salt

1 12-ounce box tricolor rotini

2 pounds medium cooked shrimp

1 cup chopped celery

1 cup (8 ounces) mayonnaise

½ cup dill pickle relish

¼ cup chopped fresh parsley leaves

3 tablespoons apple cider vinegar

1 tablespoon plus 1 teaspoon Old Bay Seasoning

1 teaspoon freshly ground black pepper

Bring a large pot of water to a boil and add the salt. Add the rotini and cook, stirring occasionally, until tender but still firm to the bite. Drain the rotini in a colander and set aside to cool. When cool, put the pasta into a serving bowl. Add the shrimp, celery, mayonnaise, relish, parsley, vinegar, 1 tablespoon Old Bay, and pepper and combine. Cover and refrigerate the salad for 1 hour before serving. Sprinkle on the remaining 1 teaspoon Old Bay before serving.

 SUPERMARKETSHORTCUTS

cooked shrimp • dill pickle relish • Old Bay Seasoning

Shrimp Creole

Sautéing the holy trinity of vegetables—celery, green peppers, and onions—is the first step when cooking so many of Louisiana's popular Creole and Cajun dishes, including Shrimp Creole. Shrimp, tomatoes, and seasonings are added to the vegetables and quickly come together in minutes. Serve this classic over a scoop of rice and dig in.

MAKES 4 SERVINGS

2 tablespoons (¼ stick) salted butter

1 cup chopped celery

1 cup frozen chopped peppers and onions

1½ pounds jumbo shrimp, peeled and deveined

1 14.5-ounce can RO*TEL Fire-Roasted Diced Tomatoes

3 tablespoons tomato paste

1 tablespoon hot sauce

1 teaspoon Cajun seasoning

2½ cups cooked white rice

2 tablespoons chopped parsley

Melt the butter in a large pot over medium-high heat. Add the celery and peppers and onions and sauté until lightly browned, about 5 minutes.

Stir in the shrimp, diced tomatoes, tomato paste, hot sauce, and Cajun seasoning. Cook, stirring frequently, until the shrimp are pink and cooked through, 3 to 4 minutes. Ladle into bowls over rice and garnish with the parsley.

 SUPERMARKETSHORTCUTS

frozen peppers and onions • RO*TEL Fire-Roasted Diced Tomatoes • Cajun seasoning

Pan-Seared Scallops
with Lemon Butter

Rich and meaty sea scallops are one to two inches in diameter, while smaller and sweeter bay scallops are tiny, about the size of a thumbnail. The secret to cooking sea scallops is to sear them quickly over high heat so they are crisp on the outside and tender within. Serve with roasted asparagus or broccoli.

MAKES 6 SERVINGS

1½ pounds sea scallops
½ teaspoon kosher salt
½ teaspoon freshly ground black
   pepper
2 teaspoons vegetable oil

3 tablespoons unsalted butter
2 tablespoons fresh lemon juice
¼ cup thinly sliced shallots
2 tablespoons chopped fresh
   parsley leaves

If necessary, remove the small side muscle from each scallop. Pat the scallops dry with paper towels. Season with the salt and pepper.

Heat the oil in a skillet over medium-high heat. Add the scallops in a single layer and leave room between them. Cook until golden brown on the outside and translucent in the center, about 2 minutes per side. Remove the scallops to a plate.

Reduce the heat to low. Add the butter, lemon juice, shallots, and parsley and whisk until the butter is melted. Return the scallops to the skillet along with any scallop juices on the plate and toss to combine. Divide the scallops and the sauce among six plates.

Steamed Mussels

Now that fresh farm-raised mussels are available at supermarket fish counters, this simple and satisfying bistro classic can be on the table faster than you can say "Bon appétit!" Mussels make a festive family or company-worthy dinner any time of the week. Bring the whole pot to the table, then remove the lid so everyone can inhale the sweet, briny aroma. Baskets of toasted garlic bread, a crisp white wine, and a ladle for scooping out the mussels and broth make this a perfect meal.

MAKES 4 SERVINGS

4 pounds mussels
2 tablespoons (¼ stick) unsalted
 butter
6 garlic cloves, sliced
½ teaspoon red pepper flakes
¾ cup dry white wine

2 tomatoes, seeded and chopped
½ teaspoon kosher salt
½ teaspoon freshly ground black
 pepper
¼ cup chopped fresh parsley leaves

Put the mussels in a colander and rinse them well under cold running water. Remove any beards and discard any broken or open mussels.

Melt the butter in a large pot over medium-high heat. Add the garlic and red pepper flakes and cook, stirring frequently, until the garlic is soft and fragrant, about 2 minutes. Add the mussels, wine, tomatoes, salt, and pepper. Increase the heat to high and cover the pot. Cook until all the mussels have opened wide, 4 to 5 minutes. Stir in the parsley. Before serving, discard any mussels that are unopened.

Noodles and More Noodles

NOODLES ARE A STAPLE FOOD IN SO MANY CUISINES. THEY CAN BE FRESH OR dried as well as flat, round, or formed into hundreds of shapes and sizes. They can be boiled, then baked; panfried; and even deep-fried. Noodles are made from wheat, buckwheat, rice, and other grains. Today we can even buy or make spiral-cut noodles from vegetables.

You don't have to spend oodles of time making noodle dishes. A baked pasta with frozen gnocchi and broccoli and vodka sauce from a jar saves you hours of prep. Unlike risotto, orzotto, made with rice-shaped pasta, requires little stirring and is done in half the amount of time as its cousin.

And remember this: There's more to noodles than Italian pasta. Quick and creamy American mac 'n' cheese comes out of the pressure cooker in just six minutes. Really. The Japanese are world famous for their soba noodle dishes with meats, vegetables, and balanced seasonings. Ya-ka Mein, a New Orleans street food made with spaghetti, broth, and Cajun seasoning, comes together in no time.

It's a noodle palooza. Start twirling and enjoy.

Baked Ziti

Spoon leftovers into individual portions in plastic containers and freeze. Reheat in the microwave for a quick meal.

MAKES 8 SERVINGS

1 tablespoon kosher salt

1 16-ounce box ziti

2 tablespoons olive oil

1 cup chopped yellow onions

4 garlic cloves, minced

2 teaspoons dried basil

½ teaspoon red pepper flakes

4 cups jarred marinara sauce

4 cups (1 pound) shredded
   mozzarella

½ cup (2 ounces) grated
   Parmigiano-Reggiano

¼ cup chopped fresh parsley leaves

Bring a large pot of water to a boil and add the salt. Add the ziti and cook, stirring until tender but still firm to the bite. Drain the ziti in a colander.

Heat the oven to 350°F.

Heat the oil in a large pot over medium heat. Add the onions, garlic, basil, and red pepper flakes. Cook until the onions are translucent, 5 to 6 minutes, stirring occasionally.

Stir in the marinara sauce, reduce the heat to low, and cook for 5 minutes. Remove the sauce from the heat, add the cooked ziti, and stir until coated.

Pour half of the ziti mixture into a 9 x 13-inch baking dish, then evenly sprinkle on 2 cups of the mozzarella and ¼ cup of the Parmigiano-Reggiano. Repeat with the remaining ziti mixture, mozzarella, and Parmigiano.

Bake until the casserole is heated through and the cheese is melted, 35 to 40 minutes. Remove from the oven, sprinkle the parsley on top, and let the casserole sit for 5 to10 minutes before serving.

SUPERMARKETSHORTCUTS

marinara sauce • shredded mozzarella

Meatball Lasagna

Here's a super-easy lasagna that eliminates time-consuming steps by using jarred tomato sauce, frozen meatballs, and no-boil lasagna noodles.

MAKES 10 SERVINGS

1 15-ounce container whole-milk ricotta

2 cups (8 ounces) plus 1½ cups (5 ounces) shredded mozzarella

¼ cup (2 ounces) plus ¼ cup (2 ounces) grated Parmigiano-Reggiano

1 large egg, lightly beaten

1 teaspoon freshly ground black pepper

1 teaspoon Italian seasoning

6 to 7 cups marinara sauce

1½ pounds cooked and frozen Italian-style meatballs, thawed and crumbled

1 9-ounce box oven-ready, no-boil lasagna noodles

Heat the oven to 350°F.

Mix the ricotta, the 2 cups mozzarella, the ¼ cup Parmigiano-Reggiano, the egg, pepper, and Italian seasoning in a bowl until combined and thick.

Mix the marinara sauce and crumbled meatballs together in a bowl. Evenly spread 1½ cups of the marinara-meatball sauce on the bottom of a 9 x 13-inch baking dish. Arrange a layer of noodles on top of the sauce. Spoon ⅓ of the ricotta mixture on the noodles. Using your fingers, spread the ricotta mixture on the noodles. Repeat the layers, finishing with the remaining marinara-meatball sauce evenly spread on top. Sprinkle with the remaining 1½ cups mozzarella and ¼ cup Parmigiano-Reggiano.

Cover the baking dish with foil and bake for 30 to 35 minutes. Remove the foil and bake for an additional 25 minutes, until heated through.

 SUPERMARKETSHORTCUTS

shredded mozzarella • Italian seasoning • marinara sauce • frozen cooked meatballs • No-boil lasagna noodles

Baked Gnocchi with Broccoli and Cheese

This rib-sticking casserole comes together in no time with a few supermarket shortcuts, including frozen gnocchi and broccoli, and vodka sauce in a jar. Top with mozzarella before putting it into the oven, and you'll have a dish that will become a household family favorite.

MAKES 4 TO 5 SERVINGS

1 pound frozen gnocchi

1 12-ounce bag frozen broccoli florets

1 24-ounce jar vodka sauce

¾ cup low-sodium chicken broth

1 teaspoon freshly ground black pepper

1 teaspoon garlic powder

½ cup (2 ounces) grated Parmigiano-Reggiano

2 cups (8 ounces) shredded mozzarella

Heat the oven to 350°F.

Combine the gnocchi, broccoli florets, vodka sauce, broth, pepper, garlic powder, and Parmigiano-Reggiano in a large bowl and toss well.

Pour the mixture into a 9 x 13 inch baking dish and distribute evenly. Sprinkle the mozzarella on top.

Bake until bubbly and the cheese is melted, about 45 minutes. Let the casserole sit for 10 minutes before serving.

SUPERMARKETSHORTCUTS

frozen gnocchi • frozen broccoli • vodka sauce • low-sodium chicken broth • shredded mozzarella

Oh-So-Easy Pressure Cooker
Mac 'n' Cheesey

Whenever mac 'n' cheese is on the lunch menu in the QVC cafeteria, I order it. One particular day, it had a complex flavor. When I was told that bacon and ranch dressing mix had been folded in, I knew I had to make it at home. Why not try it in the pressure cooker? Once the macaroni is pressure-cooked, then the other ingredients are stirred in. Here's the kicker: This version cooks in just six minutes. You can't make mac 'n' cheese from a box this fast!

MAKES 8 SERVINGS

1 pound sliced bacon, chopped

1 pound elbow macaroni

1 teaspoon ground mustard

1 teaspoon freshly ground black pepper

1 teaspoon kosher salt

1 12-ounce can evaporated milk

¾ cup milk

8 ounces Velveeta, cut into ½-inch cubes

1½ cups (6 ounces) shredded extra-sharp Cheddar

1 1-ounce packet ranch salad dressing mix

Cook the chopped bacon in a skillet over medium heat until crisp, 12 to 15 minutes. Using a slotted spoon, remove the bacon to a paper towel–lined plate.

Put 3¾ cups water, the macaroni, mustard, pepper, and salt in the pressure cooker. Stir to combine, ensuring that the macaroni is covered by water. Close the lid, set to high pressure, and cook for 6 minutes. Do a quick release.

Open the lid, add the evaporated milk, regular milk, Velveeta, Cheddar, and dressing mix. Turn the pressure cooker off and stir well to combine all. Close the lid of the pressure cooker and let sit until the cheeses are melted, about 3 minutes. Stir in the bacon before serving.

 **SUPERMARKET**SHORTCUTS

evaporated milk • dry ranch dressing mix

Pressure Cooker Rigatoni with Shredded Beef and Pesto

Rigatoni is often served with a long-simmered ground beef and tomato sauce. In this speedy version, the beef is cooked in the pressure cooker, then shredded, for a different texture than when ground beef is used. The shredded meat, uncooked rigatoni, and broth cook for a brief six minutes in the pressure cooker. Swirl in some pesto and you've got a new twist on this restaurant classic.

MAKES 6 SERVINGS

2 pounds beef chuck, cut into 1½-inch pieces
1 cup chopped yellow onions
6 garlic cloves, minced
1 cup plus 1½ cups low-sodium beef broth
½ teaspoon kosher salt

1 teaspoon freshly ground black pepper
1 pound rigatoni
1 11-ounce container pesto
⅓ cup (1½ ounces) grated Pecorino Romano
⅓ cup chopped fresh basil leaves

Put the beef, onions, garlic, the 1 cup broth, salt, and pepper in the pressure cooker. Stir to combine. Close the lid, set to high pressure, and cook for 40 minutes. Do a quick release. Remove the beef to a bowl with a slotted spoon. Using two forks, shred the beef.

Add the remaining 1½ cups broth and the rigatoni to the pressure cooker, making sure the rigatoni is covered with liquid. Place the shredded beef on top of the rigatoni. Do not stir. Close the lid, set the pressure to high, and cook for 6 minutes. Do a quick release. Stir the pesto into the pasta. Let the rigatoni sit for 2 minutes in the pressure cooker with the lid open. Stir again. Top each serving with some Pecorino Romano and basil.

SUPERMARKETSHORTCUTS
low-sodium beef broth • pesto

Bow Ties with Andouille, Peppers, and Tomatoes

Andouille sausage imparts a smoky flavor to this one-pot pasta. Top each serving with some Asiago shavings so they will melt into the warm pasta. Nutty and sharp Asiago, a cow's milk cheese from northern Italy, comes in different textures, from semi-soft to hard. To make the cheese shavings, buy a firm Asiago and use a vegetable peeler.

MAKES 6 SERVINGS

1 tablespoon plus ½ teaspoon kosher salt

1 pound bow ties

1 tablespoon olive oil

2 green bell peppers, seeded and cut into ¼-inch-thick strips

1 pound andouille sausage, sliced into ¼-inch rounds

2 14.5-ounce cans diced tomatoes with basil, garlic, and oregano

1 teaspoon freshly ground black pepper

2 ounces Asiago, shaved

Bring a large pot of water to a boil and add the 1 tablespoon salt. Add the pasta, stir occasionally, and cook until done. Drain the pasta in a colander, but do not rinse it.

Heat the oil in the same pot over medium-high heat. Add the bell peppers and sausage and cook, stirring occasionally, until the sausage is brown, 5 to 6 minutes. Stir in the tomatoes, the remaining ½ teaspoon salt, and the pepper. Reduce the heat to medium and cook until the bell peppers are soft, 6 to 8 minutes. Stir the cooked pasta into the pot and cook until heated through, stirring occasionally, 3 to 4 minutes. Sprinkle each serving with Asiago shavings.

Chicken Orzotto

As much as I love traditional risotto, I don't always have the time to stand at the stove, add the broth, and constantly stir the rice until it's cooked just right. Orzotto is made with orzo, rice-shaped pasta, rather than the Arborio rice that is called for in most risottos. It cooks in half the time and doesn't require your undivided attention. Put everything into the skillet, stir occasionally, and orzotto is ready in less than twenty minutes. Like risotto, the possible additions are endless. While I love this with chicken, feel free to replace it with shrimp or sausage.

MAKES 4 SERVINGS

2 tablespoons olive oil
1½ pounds chicken tenders
1 cup chopped yellow onions
3 garlic cloves, minced
1 teaspoon lemon and pepper
    seasoning

2¾ cups low-sodium chicken broth
1 cup orzo
¼ cup chopped fresh parsley leaves
1 teaspoon grated lemon zest
⅓ cup (1½ ounces) grated
    Parmigiano-Reggiano

Heat the oil in a large pot over medium-high heat. Add the chicken, onions, garlic, and lemon and pepper seasoning. Cook until the chicken tenders are golden brown, 6 to 8 minutes, stirring often.

Add the broth and orzo. Reduce the heat to medium, cover, and cook until the orzo is tender, 15 to 18 minutes. Stir in the parsley, lemon zest, and Parmigiano-Reggiano and serve.

 SUPERMARKETSHORTCUTS

lemon and pepper seasoning • low-sodium chicken broth

Fettuccine Alfredo

A comfort food classic with a convenient twist: Alfredo sauce from a jar. Onions, shallots, and garlic are cooked until soft, and then tossed with the sauce and long, flat fettuccine pasta for creamy deliciousness. Make this an even heartier meal by adding some cooked chicken or shrimp—or my favorite, crumbled cooked bacon.

MAKES 6 SERVINGS

1 tablespoon kosher salt, plus
  ½ teaspoon kosher salt
1 pound fettuccine
2 tablespoons extra-virgin olive oil
1 cup chopped yellow onions
3 tablespoons chopped shallots
4 garlic cloves, minced

1 15-ounce jar Alfredo sauce
1 teaspoon freshly ground black
  pepper
½ cup (2 ounces) grated Pecorino
  Romano
¼ cup chopped fresh parsley leaves

Bring a large pot of water to a boil and add the 1 tablespoon salt. Add the fettuccine and cook, stirring until tender but still firm to the bite. Reserve 1 cup of the pasta cooking water, then drain the fettuccine in a colander but do not rinse.

Heat the oil over medium-low heat in the same pot the fettuccine was cooked in. Add the onions, shallots, garlic, and the remaining ½ teaspoon salt, and cook, stirring frequently, until the onions are translucent, 5 to 6 minutes. Stir in the Alfredo sauce, reserved pasta cooking water, and pepper. Cook until the sauce is hot, 3 to 4 minutes. Add the cooked fettuccine and stir to coat the pasta with the sauce. Divide the fettuccine among six bowls and then sprinkle on the Pecorino Romano and parsley.

 **SUPERMARKET**SHORTCUT

Alfredo sauce

Soba Noodles

Soba means "buckwheat" in Japanese. Like Italian pasta, thin, chewy soba noodles can be served hot or cold with a variety of meats, vegetables, and seasonings. Unlike for pasta, no salt is added to the cooking water and the noodles must be rinsed once cooked to keep them from becoming gummy.

MAKES 4 TO 6 SERVINGS

1 8-ounce package soba noodles
1 tablespoon plus 2 tablespoons vegetable oil
1 red bell pepper, seeded and chopped
1 cup shredded carrots
1 cup chopped scallions

1 cup cooked edamame
6 garlic cloves, minced
2 tablespoons minced fresh ginger
1¼ cups stir-fry teriyaki sauce/ marinade
2 tablespoons sesame seeds

Bring a pot of water to a boil. Add the soba noodles. Once the water comes back to a boil, stir the noodles, then reduce the heat to a simmer. Cooking times can vary, so check the package directions, but the range is usually between 5 and 7 minutes. Taste a noodle; it should be fully cooked but not mushy. Drain the noodles in a colander, then run them under cool water and drain again. Let the noodles sit in the colander for a few minutes, then put them in a bowl and toss with the 1 tablespoon oil to coat completely.

Heat the remaining 2 tablespoons oil in a large pot over medium heat. Add the bell pepper, carrots, scallions, edamame, garlic, and ginger. Cook, stirring occasionally, until the vegetables are cooked but still crunchy, about 5 minutes.

Reduce the heat to low and add the teriyaki sauce/marinade and noodles. Cook, stirring constantly, until the noodles are heated through and coated with the sauce. Sprinkle with the sesame seeds before serving.

 SUPERMARKETSHORTCUTS

soba noodles • stir-fry teriyaki sauce/marinade

Ya-Ka Mein

No matter what time of year you visit New Orleans, a festival is held every week-end to celebrate the Crescent City's vibrant food, history, or musical heritage. Food stalls line the streets and offer local favorites, such as gumbo, po' boys, and Ya-Ka Mein, a Chinese American–Creole beef noodle soup that is believed to have originated in New Orleans in the 1950s. The soup is also called "Old Sober," because many people believe in its restorative powers after a night of partying.

MAKES 6 SERVINGS

12 ounces spaghetti
2 tablespoons olive oil
6 cups low-sodium beef broth
1 teaspoon Cajun seasoning
1 pound beef sirloin, thinly sliced
1½ tablespoons soy sauce

1½ tablespoons ketchup
1 tablespoon hot sauce
3 hard-boiled eggs, halved
   lengthwise
⅓ cup chopped fresh chives

Bring a large pot of water to a boil. Add the spaghetti, stir occasionally, and cook until tender but still firm to the bite. Drain the spaghetti in a colander and place the spaghetti in a bowl.

Add the olive oil and toss until the spaghetti is coated. Divide the spaghetti among six bowls. Set aside.

Put the broth and Cajun seasoning in a large pot and bring to a boil. Add the beef and cook until it is no longer pink, 2 to 3 minutes. Using tongs, remove the beef from the broth and add to the bowls with the noodles. Stir the soy sauce, ketchup, and hot sauce into the broth and simmer for 1 minute.

Ladle the broth into soup bowls. Place 1 egg half in each bowl and then sprinkle with some of the chives.

 SUPERMARKETSHORTCUTS

low-sodium beef broth · Cajun seasoning · hot sauce · hard-boiled eggs

Sides

A SIDE DISH IS LIKE A SUPPORTING ACTOR IN A FILM, BUT IT STILL NEEDS superstar taste. Sides aren't there to just fill out a meal. Depending on what you make, sides can complement and enhance the main dish, or they can serve as a contrast. They make meals sing. If your main dish is creamy, pair it with something that has a different texture, such as Pan-Grilled Asparagus with Red Peppers, Feta, and Olives. A plain main like beef or pork tenderloin calls for sides that are more complex in flavor, like Roasted Potatoes with Bacon and Ranch Dressing. There are endless possibilities. Consider the sweet and nutty flavor of Roasted and Glazed Butternut Squash, or the meatiness of Whole Roasted Cauliflower or Roasted Tomatoes with Corn Salsa. It's time to let your side dishes take starring roles.

Roasted and Glazed
Butternut Squash

Now that butternut squash cubes can be found in produce sections, gone are the days when you have to get out a jackhammer to cut the squash and dig out the seeds. This easy side tosses precut squash cubes with brown sugar, butter, a little salt and pepper, and herbs before roasting. When you bite into each piece, the squash is caramelized on the outside and soft on the inside.

Sometimes the squash cubes from the grocery store come in large 2-inch chunks, so I cut them into smaller 1-inch pieces for faster cooking.

MAKES 6 SERVINGS

6 tablespoons unsalted butter
¼ cup (packed) light brown sugar
1 teaspoon minced fresh thyme leaves
1 teaspoon kosher salt

½ teaspoon freshly ground black pepper
2 pounds butternut squash, peeled and cut into 1-inch cubes
1 tablespoon minced fresh sage leaves

Heat the oven to 425°F. Line a sheet pan with aluminum foil.

Put the butter, brown sugar, thyme, salt, and pepper in a saucepan over medium heat. Cook, stirring occasionally, until the butter is melted and the sugar is dissolved.

Put the butternut squash in a bowl. Add the glaze and toss to coat.

Arrange the butternut squash on the prepared pan in a single layer. Bake until tender and golden brown, 25 to 30 minutes; do not toss or stir the squash as it cooks. Transfer the squash to a serving bowl and sprinkle the sage on top.

 **SUPERMARKET**SHORTCUT
butternut squash cubes

Roasted Potatoes with Bacon and Ranch Dressing

I do love my ranch dressing, especially when it comes in handy little packets. Toss red-skinned potatoes with the seasoning and roast them in the oven and they become crisp and savory on the outside and soothingly creamy on the inside.

MAKES 6 SERVINGS

Vegetable oil spray
2½ pounds red-skinned potatoes, quartered
2 tablespoons olive oil
1 1-ounce packet dry ranch salad dressing mix

½ teaspoon freshly ground black pepper
1 pound bacon, chopped
2 tablespoons chopped fresh chives
Sour cream (optional)

Heat the oven to 425°F. Line a sheet pan with aluminum foil and coat the foil with vegetable oil spray.

Put the potatoes, oil, ranch dressing mix, and pepper in a bowl and toss to coat.

Arrange the potatoes, skin side down, on the sheet pan in a single layer. Bake until golden brown and tender when pierced with a knife, 45 to 50 minutes. Do not toss or stir the potatoes as they cook.

While the potatoes are roasting, cook the bacon in a skillet over medium heat until crisp, 12 to 15 minutes. Remove to paper towels using a slotted spoon. Reserve 2 tablespoons of the bacon fat.

Put the roasted potatoes in a bowl and toss with the bacon, chives, and reserved bacon fat before serving with sour cream on the side, if desired.

 **SUPERMARKET**SHORTCUT

dry ranch salad dressing mix

Garlic

Peeling garlic cloves when you need a lot of them is time-consuming. You can buy already peeled garlic in a container or a bag or try the following hack: Put a whole head of garlic in a jar or plastic container. Cover with the lid and shake the jar vigorously for 20 to 30 seconds. Pour the garlic out and remove the cloves from the papery skins. The garlic cloves are now ready to slice, dice, or mince.

Garlic Lovers Smashed Potatoes

Mashed potatoes are perfect with just about everything. My version has just the right amount of garlic. I boil the garlic with the potatoes and then rough-mash the cloves into the mixture. The result is creamy goodness and just enough garlic, so everyone asks for seconds.

MAKES 6 SERVINGS

2½ pounds Yukon Gold potatoes, halved

16 garlic cloves, peeled and halved lengthwise

2 teaspoons plus 1 teaspoon kosher salt

¾ cup milk

⅓ cup (2½ ounces) sour cream

4 tablespoons (½ stick) unsalted butter, softened

1 teaspoon freshly ground black pepper

⅓ cup chopped scallions

Put the potatoes, garlic, and the 2 teaspoons salt in a large pot. Add cold water to cover the potatoes by 1 inch. Bring to a boil, reduce the heat to medium, and simmer until the potatoes can be pierced with a fork, 25 to 30 minutes.

Drain the potatoes and garlic in a colander and put them into a bowl. Add the milk, sour cream, butter, pepper, and the remaining 1 teaspoon salt to the potatoes. With an electric mixer on low speed, smash the potatoes and garlic until all the ingredients are combined, 35 to 45 seconds. The potatoes should have chunks, so don't overmix them. Top with the scallions before serving. (If made ahead, put the potatoes back in the pot and reheat over low heat, stirring occasionally.)

SUPERMARKETSHORTCUT

peeled garlic cloves

Sweet Potato Home Fries

I've always loved home fries as a side dish, so I got to wondering how I could use sweet, rather than white, potatoes and stay true to the original cooking method. Pair these home fries with breakfast or a steak dinner.

MAKES 4 SERVINGS

1½ pounds sweet potatoes, peeled and cut into ½-inch pieces
2 tablespoons vegetable oil
1 cup chopped yellow onions
1 green bell pepper, seeded and chopped

4 garlic cloves, minced
1 teaspoon paprika
1 teaspoon kosher salt
½ teaspoon freshly ground black pepper
¼ cup thinly sliced scallions

Put the sweet potatoes in a large pot and add 8 cups cold water. Bring to a boil, reduce the heat to medium, and cook until just tender but still firm when pierced with a knife, 5 to 6 minutes. Do not overcook. Drain the potatoes and set aside.

Heat the oil in a large skillet over medium heat. Add the onions and bell pepper, then cook, stirring occasionally, until the onions are translucent, 5 to 6 minutes. Increase the heat to high, then stir in the sweet potatoes, garlic, paprika, salt, and pepper. Cook, stirring occasionally, until the potatoes are browned, 8 to 10 minutes. Top with the scallions before serving.

Whole Roasted Cauliflower

Roasting a whole head of cauliflower is a time saver because you don't have to cut the vegetable into florets. Just spread a seasoned yogurt mixture on the entire head, put it in the oven, and in an hour, you'll have a crusty-on-the-outside, tender-on-the-inside side dish. For a dramatic presentation, bring the whole cauliflower to the table on a plate with a fork and knife for easy slicing.

MAKES 6 TO 8 SERVINGS

1 large head cauliflower
¼ cup nonfat plain Greek yogurt
2 tablespoons Dijon mustard
1 tablespoon honey
1 teaspoon garlic powder
1 teaspoon onion powder
½ teaspoon kosher salt

Heat the oven to 425°F. Line a sheet pan with aluminum foil.

Remove any outer leaves of the cauliflower and trim the stem so the head of cauliflower sits flat.

Whisk together the yogurt, mustard, honey, garlic powder, onion powder, and salt in a bowl.

Using clean hands or a pastry brush, evenly smear the yogurt mixture all over the cauliflower. Place the cauliflower, stem side down, on the prepared sheet pan. Bake until the exterior is golden brown and the interior can be easily pierced with a knife, 55 minutes to 1 hour. Slice the cauliflower into wedges to serve.

Pan-Grilled Asparagus with Red Peppers, Feta, and Olives

Asparagus grilled on the cooktop and jarred roasted red peppers are combined with salty feta and briny olives in this colorful vegetable platter. Serve as a first course, as a side dish with lamb or chicken, or as a vegetarian main course.

MAKES 4 SERVINGS

⅓ cup jarred roasted and sliced red peppers

⅓ cup pitted Kalamata olives

⅓ cup Greek or Italian bottled salad dressing

1 pound fresh asparagus, trimmed

2 tablespoons extra-virgin olive oil

½ teaspoon kosher salt

½ teaspoon freshly ground black pepper

⅓ cup feta cheese crumbles

Stir the red peppers, olives, and dressing together in a bowl.

Put the asparagus in a shallow dish. Add the olive oil, salt, and pepper to the asparagus and toss to coat evenly.

Heat a grill pan over medium-high heat. Put the asparagus crosswise into the pan and cook, turning occasionally, until lightly charred and cooked through, 8 to 10 minutes.

Put the cooked asparagus on a serving platter. Drizzle with the pepper-olive dressing. Sprinkle the feta cheese crumbles on top and serve.

 SUPERMARKETSHORTCUTS

roasted and sliced red peppers • Greek or Italian bottled salad dressing • feta cheese crumbles

Roasted Tomatoes
with Corn Salsa

Scoop out the insides of large, juicy summer tomatoes. Once seasoned and filled with a mixture of corn, cheese, salsa, and bread stuffing, all they need is half an hour in the oven. It's easy to become a member of the clean-plate club with this savory side, because you even get to eat the bowl!

MAKES 8 SERVINGS

4 large tomatoes
1 teaspoon kosher salt
1 teaspoon freshly ground black pepper
1½ cups frozen corn kernels, thawed

1 cup dry country-style cubed bread stuffing
1 cup jarred salsa
1 cup shredded pepper Jack
¼ cup chopped fresh cilantro leaves
2 teaspoons ground cumin

Heat the oven to 375°F.

Cut a thin slice off the top of each tomato; scoop out the insides and discard along with the tops. Place the hollowed-out tomatoes, cut side down, on paper towels and drain for 5 minutes. Turn the tomatoes over and season the inside of each one with salt and pepper.

Combine the corn, stuffing, salsa, cheese, cilantro, and cumin in a bowl. Spoon the mixture into the seasoned tomato cavities.

Put the stuffed tomatoes in an 8 x 8-inch baking dish. Bake for 30 to 35 minutes, or until the tomatoes are tender when pierced with a knife and the stuffing is heated through. Let cool for 5 minutes before cutting in half to serve.

 SUPERMARKETSHORTCUTS
frozen corn kernels • bread stuffing cubes • jarred salsa

Mexican Street Corn Off the Cob

Mexican street corn is traditionally roasted over an open grill to give it a nice char, then brushed with a smear of mayonnaise and a drizzle of cotija cheese. I figured why not take the corn *off* the cob, toss it with those same ingredients, and serve it as a warm or room-temperature side dish? Cotija, a dry, crumbly Mexican cheese with a creamy texture and salty finish, can be found in the cheese case. Some markets sell frozen roasted corn kernels, but for this dish, fresh corn is best.

MAKES 6 SERVINGS

8 ears corn

2 tablespoons vegetable oil

⅓ cup (2½ ounces) mayonnaise

2½ tablespoons fresh lime juice

1 tablespoon smoked paprika

½ teaspoon freshly ground black pepper

½ cup crumbled cotija or feta crumbles

¼ cup chopped fresh cilantro leaves

½ teaspoon red pepper flakes (optional)

To remove the corn from the cobs, use a corn stripper. Or hold the cob at a slight angle with a kitchen towel underneath it for stability, and then slice the corn off from top to bottom.

Heat the oil in a skillet over medium-high heat. Add the corn kernels and cook, without stirring, until the corn is lightly charred on one side, about 5 minutes. Stir and continue to cook until the kernels are charred all over and cooked through, 6 to 8 minutes. Place the cooked corn in a bowl. Stir in the mayonnaise, lime juice, smoked paprika, and black pepper and toss to combine. Spoon the corn mixture into a serving bowl and top with the cotija, cilantro, and red pepper flakes, if using.

SUPERMARKETSHORTCUT

feta cheese crumbles

Southern Succotash Stir-Fry

You might be surprised to learn that succotash, a simple corn and bean dish, is originally from New England. As succotash made its way to the South, cooks added bacon, tomatoes, and other ingredients. Mine is cooked in rendered bacon fat. Traditionally served in the summer with fresh corn kernels and shelled lima beans, you can make a year-round version with frozen corn and beans. For a pop of color, I add some diced bell peppers.

MAKES 6 SERVINGS

8 ounces bacon, chopped into small pieces

1½ cups frozen corn kernels, thawed

1½ cups chopped sweet onions, such as Vidalia or Walla Walla

1 red bell pepper, seeded and chopped

1 teaspoon kosher salt

1 teaspoon freshly ground black pepper

1 pound frozen lima beans, cooked according to package instructions and drained

2 tablespoons white vinegar

2 tablespoons minced fresh parsley leaves

Put the bacon in a skillet over medium heat and cook until crispy, 12 to 15 minutes, stirring occasionally. Remove to a paper towel–lined plate with a slotted spoon, leaving the bacon fat in the skillet.

Add the corn, onions, bell pepper, salt, and black pepper to the skillet. Cook until the onions are translucent and the bell pepper is tender, 5 to 6 minutes. Stir in the lima beans, cooked bacon, vinegar, and parsley. Toss to combine and heat through, then serve.

SUPERMARKETSHORTCUTS

frozen corn kernels • frozen lima beans

Panade

A panade is a savory casserole that combines all the best parts of French onion soup. In my version, stale bread cubes are arranged in a baking dish, covered with spinach and canned French onion soup, showered with cheese, and then baked. Serve on its own or as a hearty side with beef, poultry, or chicken.

MAKES 10 TO 12 SERVINGS

Vegetable oil spray
4 tablespoons (½ stick) unsalted butter
1 1-pound bag frozen cut-leaf spinach, thawed and squeezed dry
6 garlic cloves, minced
1 teaspoon freshly ground black pepper

2 10½-ounce cans condensed French onion soup
1 16- to 18-ounce loaf stale crusty artisanal bread (2 to 3 days old), cut into 1-inch chunks
2½ cups (10 ounces) shredded Gouda

Heat the oven to 350°F. Coat a 9 x 13-inch baking dish with vegetable oil spray.

Melt the butter in a skillet over medium heat. Stir in the spinach, garlic, and pepper. Cook until heated through, about 5 minutes.

Pour the onion soup and 1 cup water into a saucepan and heat over medium heat.

Arrange half of the bread in the prepared dish. Distribute the spinach mixture on top of the bread. Top with 1 cup of the Gouda, followed by the remaining bread. Pour the soup mixture over the bread mixture. Sprinkle the remaining 1½ cups Gouda on top. Let the panade sit for 5 minutes so the bread can absorb most of the liquid.

Cover the baking dish with foil. Bake for 30 minutes. Remove the foil and bake for an additional 20 minutes, until the panade is bubbling. Let it rest for 5 minutes before serving.

 **SUPERMARKET**SHORTCUTS

frozen cut-leaf spinach • condensed French onion soup

Air-Frying

BOY, DO I LOVE USING MY AIR FRYER. I CAN ENJOY CRISP CHICKEN WINGS, bacon, vegetables, fritters, hand pies, donuts, and more—without the mess of deep-frying or the guilt. With deep-frying, a pot of cooking oil has to be brought to a specific hot temperature. The oil splatters easily, you have to figure out a safe way to discard it once it cools, and the cooked food needs to be drained on paper towels to get rid of excess oil. And let's not even mention the calories in fried foods.

This remarkable appliance has an internal fan that rapidly circulates heated air, rather than hot oil, around food. The air fryer is safe and easy to use. Some recipes in this chapter use just a misting of vegetable oil spray or none at all. Just set the machine for cooking time and temperature, put the food in, and press Start. In minutes, you'll have chicken nuggets, empanadas, and banana spring rolls.

For these recipes, I use a 3.4-quart digital air fryer that comes with a frying basket and a 6 x 3-inch round cake pan (also called a barrel) that fits right in the cooking basket. You'll need that cake pan to make the Apple-Blueberry Cobbler.

Honey-Bourbon Chicken Wings

Chicken wings have three parts: the meaty drumettes, the wingettes (or flats) with two bones, and the tips that contain bone and cartilage but no meat. These days, it's easy to find packages of separate drumettes and wingettes, so you don't have to spend time cutting up the wings. This recipe is a tangy, sweet alternative to hot wings.

MAKES 2 SERVINGS

¼ **cup bourbon**
¼ **cup honey**
3 **tablespoons tomato paste**
2 **tablespoons (¼ stick) salted
    butter**
¾ **teaspoon onion powder**

¼ **teaspoon plus 1 teaspoon
    kosher salt**
¼ **teaspoon plus 1 teaspoon fresh
    ground black pepper**
2 **pounds chicken drumettes and
    wingettes**

Whisk together the bourbon, honey, tomato paste, butter, onion powder, the ¼ teaspoon salt, and the ¼ teaspoon pepper in a saucepan. Bring to a boil, then reduce the heat to a simmer. Cook for 8 minutes, stirring occasionally.

Season the chicken with the remaining 1 teaspoon salt and 1 teaspoon pepper.

Put the wings in the frying basket. Set the air fryer to 400°F and cook for 22 to 25 minutes, shaking the basket a couple of times during the cooking process.

Put the cooked wings into a serving bowl and pour the sauce on top, stirring to completely coat. Place the wings back into the basket and air-fry until the sauce is browned, about 3 minutes. Add the wings back to the bowl with any remaining sauce and toss before serving.

 **SUPERMARKET**SHORTCUT

drumettes and wingettes

Mini English-Muffin Pizzas

What kid (or adult) doesn't love a personal pizza? Pop these treats into the air fryer as soon as you hear the kids get off the school bus. By the time they drop their backpacks and hug the dog, you can have a hot snack ready for them. Then, remind them that it's homework time.

MAKES 2 SERVINGS

¼ cup jarred pizza sauce
1 English muffin, split
½ teaspoon Italian seasoning

¼ cup (1 ounce) shredded
   mozzarella
26 slices pepperoni minis

Spread the pizza sauce on both cut halves of the English muffin. Sprinkle the Italian seasoning, mozzarella, and pepperoni minis equally on each muffin half.

Set the air fryer to 380°F. Put the muffins in the frying basket. Cook until the cheese is melted and golden brown, 5 to 6 minutes.

 SUPERMARKETSHORTCUTS

pizza sauce • English muffins • Italian seasoning • shredded mozzarella • pepperoni minis

Mashed Potato-Bacon Bombs

The ease of leftovers makes this snack come together in no time at all. How much of the instant mashed potatoes to add will depend on how thick or creamy your leftover mashed potatoes are. There should be just enough to allow the leftover mashed potatoes to form a ball and not become too dense.

MAKES 18 TO 20 PIECES

1 pound bacon, chopped
2 cups leftover mashed potatoes
¾ cup instant mashed potato mix
½ cup (2 ounces) shredded Monterey Jack
2 large eggs

½ teaspoon freshly ground black pepper
¼ cup all-purpose flour
1¼ cups panko (Japanese bread crumbs)
Vegetable oil spray
Bottled ranch dressing, for dipping

Cook the chopped bacon in a skillet over medium heat until crisp, 12 to 15 minutes. Remove to a bowl using a slotted spoon. Discard the bacon fat.

Put the mashed potatoes, instant potato mix, cheese, 1 egg, and the pepper in a bowl and stir to combine. Put the flour in a shallow bowl. Beat the remaining egg with 2 tablespoons water in another bowl. Put the panko in a third shallow bowl.

Using clean hands, divide the potato mixture and shape into 18 to 20 balls. Coat the potato balls evenly with the flour, then the egg mixture, followed by the panko, shaking off any excess mixture and pressing gently to coat. Lightly spray the potato balls with the vegetable oil spray. Put half of the potato balls into the cooking basket. Set the air fryer to 380°F and cook until golden brown on the outside, shaking the basket after 5 minutes. Cook for another 5 minutes. Repeat to cook the remaining potato balls. Serve with the ranch dressing.

SUPERMARKETSHORTCUTS

instant mashed potatoes • panko • bottled ranch dressing

Chicken Nuggets with Honey Mustard and Pretzel Crumbs

Pretzels and honey mustard are a perfect pairing. Add chicken, and you've got a trio worth talking about. Pieces of chicken are dipped in flour, then honey mustard sauce, and finally crushed pretzels for a crunchy, salty crust. The crisp air-fried nuggets are served with the remaining honey mustard sauce for dipping.

MAKES 4 SERVINGS

50 to 60 mini pretzels
¾ cup plus ½ cup honey mustard sauce
2 tablespoons all-purpose flour
1 teaspoon kosher salt
½ teaspoon freshly ground pepper
1 pound boneless, skinless chicken breasts, cut into 1½-inch pieces
Vegetable oil spray

Put the pretzels in a food processor and pulse until finely crushed. Put the crushed pretzels in a shallow bowl. Pour the ¾ cup honey mustard sauce into another shallow bowl. Whisk together the flour, salt, and pepper in a third shallow bowl.

Dip each chicken nugget into the flour mixture to coat evenly. Then coat each nugget with the honey mustard sauce, shaking off any excess, then coat with the pretzel crumbs.

Lightly spray the frying basket with vegetable oil spray. Working in batches, put some of the chicken nuggets into the basket in a single layer. Air-fry at 350°F for 12 minutes. Repeat with the remaining chicken nuggets. Serve with the remaining ½ cup honey mustard sauce for dipping.

SUPERMARKETSHORTCUTS

mini pretzels • honey mustard sauce

Beef Empanadas

Empanadas are traditionally deep-fried in oil, but my version uses none. Make a double batch. Believe me, they're that good.

MAKES 4 SERVINGS

4 ounces ground beef
2 tablespoons minced yellow onion
2 garlic cloves, minced
1 tablespoon tomato paste
¾ teaspoon kosher salt
¾ teaspoon freshly ground black pepper

¾ teaspoon ground cumin
½ teaspoon dried oregano
1 refrigerated pie crust, at room temperature
1 large egg, beaten

Put the beef, onion, garlic, tomato paste, salt, pepper, cumin, and oregano in a skillet over medium heat. Sauté, breaking up the meat with a spoon, until the beef is browned and crumbled, 4 to 5 minutes. Remove the skillet from the heat and let cool.

Unroll the pie crust. Using a small bowl or cookie cutter, cut out three 5-inch circles. Shape the excess dough into a ball. Use a rolling pin to roll out the dough and cut one more circle.

Spoon 2½ tablespoons of the beef mixture into the middle of each circle. Brush the edges of the pastry with the beaten egg. Fold each circle. Using a fork, press the edge to crimp and seal the empanadas. Lightly brush each empanada with the beaten egg.

Put 2 empanadas in the frying basket and slide the basket into the air fryer. Set the temperature to 350°F and cook for 8 minutes. Turn the empanadas over and cook until golden brown, an additional 6 minutes. Repeat with the 2 remaining empanadas.

 **SUPERMARKET**SHORTCUT

refrigerated pie crust

Shredded Chicken Taquitos

A taquito, which means "small taco" in Spanish, is a small tortilla filled with chicken or beef and some cheese and then deep-fried. All that messy oil and those extra calories are avoided when an air fryer is used. Taquitos make great appetizers or the centerpiece for a Mexican-themed meal.

MAKES 4 SERVINGS

⅓ cup plain nonfat Greek yogurt
½ cup Mexican salsa verde
3 tablespoons chopped fresh cilantro
1 tablespoon fresh lime juice

2 cups shredded rotisserie or leftover cooked chicken
2 tablespoons Mexican seasoning
8 tablespoons (½ cup) shredded Monterey Jack
8 6-inch flour tortillas

Whisk together the yogurt, salsa verde, cilantro, and lime juice in a bowl. In another bowl, toss the shredded chicken with the Mexican seasoning until well coated.

Place ¼ cup of the chicken mixture and 1 tablespoon cheese on ½ of a flour tortilla. Roll up tightly and place seam side down on a plate. Repeat with the remaining tortillas.

Put 4 taquitos in a single layer, seam side down, into the frying basket. Air-fry at 375°F for 6 minutes. Using tongs, turn the taquitos over and air-fry for 4 minutes, until light golden brown. Cook the remaining 4 taquitos. Serve with the yogurt dipping sauce.

 SUPERMARKETSHORTCUTS

Mexican salsa verde • rotisserie chicken • Mexican seasoning

Fried Rice

I was curious to find out if fried rice could be made in the air fryer. It can. It's delicious. And it's made without any cooking oil. Leftover take-out rice is combined with soy and oyster sauces along with one ingredient you might not expect: Spam. Your family will love this side dish.

MAKES 4 SERVINGS

1¾ cups cooked white rice

1 8-ounce can pineapple chunks, drained

1 7-ounce can Spam®, diced

¾ cup frozen peas and carrots, thawed

¼ cup low-sodium soy sauce

3 tablespoons oyster sauce

2 teaspoons minced fresh ginger

¼ cup chopped scallions

Combine the rice, pineapple, Spam, peas and carrots, soy and oyster sauces, and ginger in a bowl. Put the mixture in a 6 x 3-inch round cake pan. Put the pan into the air fryer. Set the air fryer to 350°F and cook for 20 minutes, stirring the mixture after 10 minutes. Stir in the scallions before serving.

 SUPERMARKETSHORTCUTS

pineapple chunks • Spam • frozen peas and carrots • oyster sauce

Brussels Sprouts

You read that correctly. You know how I feel about Brussels sprouts; they're not my fave vegetable, to say the least. But so many of my foodie friends really love them, so I thought: Why not try air-frying them for a crisp texture? The sweet-spicy sauce balances the sprouts' strong flavor, so even the pickiest eater will give these a try.

MAKES 4 SERVINGS

½ cup apricot preserves

2 tablespoons Sriracha

2 tablespoons apple cider vinegar

½ teaspoon plus ½ teaspoon
    kosher salt

½ teaspoon plus ½ teaspoon fresh
    ground black pepper

1¼ pounds Brussels sprouts, stems
    trimmed and halved

1½ teaspoons vegetable oil

Whisk together the apricot preserves, Sriracha, vinegar, the ½ teaspoon salt, and the ½ teaspoon pepper in a bowl.

Put the sprouts, the oil, the remaining ½ teaspoon salt and ½ teaspoon pepper in another bowl and toss to coat. Put the sprouts into the frying basket. Set the air fryer to 400°F and cook until the sprouts are tender, 15 to 17 minutes, shaking the basket every 5 minutes. Pierce the sprouts with a knife to test for doneness. They should be tender, but not soft. Put them in the bowl with the sauce and toss well to coat.

SUPERMARKETSHORTCUTS

apricot preserves • Sriracha

Apple-Blueberry Cobbler

Given its name, you might not expect to be able to bake this dessert in an air fryer, but remember, this small appliance is actually a convection oven. Sweet treats, like this moist, fruity cobbler, can be "baked" in just minutes. The baking pan size is perfect when you want a dessert that will feed four people.

MAKES 4 SERVINGS

2⅓ cups (2 apples) Golden Delicious apples, skin on, cored, and cut into ½-inch chunks

⅔ cup fresh blueberries

3 tablespoons light brown sugar

2 teaspoons ground cinnamon

1 tablespoon fresh lemon juice

1 cup all-purpose flour

4 tablespoons sugar

⅛ teaspoon table salt

7 tablespoons cold unsalted butter, cut into ½-inch pieces

Combine the apple pieces, blueberries, brown sugar, cinnamon, and lemon juice in a bowl. Toss to coat evenly. Pour the fruit mixture into a 6 x 3-inch round cake pan.

Whisk together the flour, sugar, and salt in a bowl. Add the butter and 1 table-spoon cold water and, using your fingertips, rub the mixture together until crumbly. Sprinkle the mixture evenly over the fruit and press down lightly.

Set the air fryer to 325°F and cook for 30 to 35 minutes until golden brown. Spoon the cobbler into serving bowls.

Banana Spring Rolls with Peanut Butter–Chocolate Sauce

Sugared bananas are rolled up in egg roll wrappers, air-fried, and served with a peanut-y and chocolate-y dipping sauce.

MAKES 4 SERVINGS

⅓ cup (packed) dark brown sugar

⅓ cup granulated sugar

4 bananas, peeled and sliced into 3-inch pieces

8 egg roll wrappers

Vegetable oil spray

½ cup peanut butter–chocolate spread

1 tablespoon unsalted butter

2 tablespoons chocolate syrup

Confectioners' sugar

Whisk together the brown and granulated sugars in a bowl until evenly combined. One at a time, add the banana pieces to the sugars, pressing the sugars into the banana slices and then put them on a plate.

Arrange the egg roll wrappers on a flat surface. Using your fingertips, wet the edges of each wrapper with water. Place 1 banana piece on the upper half of a wrapper, fold in the sides, and roll tightly, making sure the seam is closed. Repeat with the remaining wrappers and bananas.

Lightly spray the air fryer basket with the vegetable oil spray. Put 4 rolls into the basket in a single layer. Air-fry the rolls at 350°F for 6 minutes. Using tongs, turn the hot rolls and air-fry until golden brown and crispy, about 3 minutes. Remove the banana rolls to a plate and repeat with the remaining ones.

Combine the peanut butter–chocolate spread, butter, and chocolate syrup in a saucepan over medium heat, stirring constantly until melted, about 3 minutes. Sprinkle the banana rolls with confectioners' sugar and serve with the sauce.

 SUPERMARKETSHORTCUTS

egg roll wrappers • peanut butter-chocolate spread • chocolate syrup

Desserts

IT CAN BE SO GRATIFYING TO SPEND AN AFTERNOON IN THE KITCHEN CREATing a stunning multilayer cake complete with filling, icing, and decorations. Or perhaps individual tartlets with homemade pie dough, a curd filling, and a meringue topping. Then there are those times when you realize, "Oops, company's coming!" or "Oh no, I need a dessert for tonight!" and there's just not enough time to make a sweet sensation from scratch. Not to worry—my simple recipes and supermarket shortcuts will come to your rescue.

With store-bought pie and graham cracker pie crusts, boxed cake mixes, packaged cookies, ice cream, and whipped toppings, you'll be able to make dinner and still have time to make not just a dessert but a dessert that is spectacular—an applause-worthy way to end a meal whether it's a simple weeknight family supper or a weekend special dinner for friends. Whatever kind of meal these desserts are for, these recipes will not disappoint. In fact, I pretty much can guarantee that even when your friends and family tell you dinner was so fabulous that they cannot possibly eat another bite, you know that everybody will have room for one of these heavenly delights. And probably even seconds.

Melted Strawberry Ice Cream Cake

Who would have ever thought that you could make a happy-dance-worthy cake with a boxed mix, three eggs, and some melted ice cream? Oh. My. Word. This easy cake is strawberry through and through: strawberry ice cream in the cake and fresh strawberries for the garnish. But imagine the endless possibilities. Chocolate chip ice cream cake with a mocha drizzle. Rocky road ice cream and chocolate marshmallows for decoration. You get the idea.

A couple of tips: Whatever flavor ice cream you choose, melt it and then measure two cups. Also, this cake must be baked in a well-greased Bundt pan.

MAKES 10 TO 12 SERVINGS

Cake

Vegetable oil spray
1 box strawberry cake mix
2 cups melted strawberry ice cream
3 large eggs

Glaze

¾ cup confectioners' sugar
4 teaspoons milk

6 fresh strawberries, halved

To make the cake, heat the oven to 350°F. Generously coat a Bundt pan with vegetable oil spray. Put the cake mix, melted ice cream, and eggs in the bowl of an electric mixer. Mix on medium speed until the batter is thick and well blended. Evenly pour the batter into the prepared pan.

Bake the cake for 30 to 35 minutes, or until a toothpick inserted in several places comes out clean. Remove the cake from the oven and let cool on a wire rack for 30 minutes. Invert the cake onto a serving plate and let cool completely.

To make the glaze, whisk together the confectioners' sugar and milk in a bowl until smooth and without any lumps. Pour the glaze on the cake, making sure it drizzles all over. Garnish with the strawberries.

SUPERMARKETSHORTCUTS

strawberry cake mix • strawberry ice cream

Slow Cooker Chocolate Pudding Cake

People are often surprised to learn that delectable desserts can be made in the slow cooker. This luscious cake has the consistency of creamy pudding and is a chocolate lover's idea of heaven. If you love peanut butter as much as I do, top the cake with some peanut butter chips.

MAKES 10 SERVINGS

2 cup all-purpose flour
4 teaspoons baking powder
1 cup (2 sticks) salted butter
6 ounces 60% cocoa bittersweet chocolate, chopped
1¼ cups plus ½ cup granulated sugar

6 tablespoons plus ⅔ cup Dutch-processed cocoa powder
2 tablespoons pure vanilla extract
2 large egg yolks
⅔ cup light brown sugar
3 cups hot brewed coffee

Whisk together the flour and baking powder in a bowl. Set aside.

Melt the butter and chocolate together in a double boiler over simmering water. Remove the bowl from the heat and whisk in the 1¼ cups sugar, the 6 tablespoons cocoa powder, the vanilla, and egg yolks until fully incorporated. Add the flour mixture and stir with a spatula until combined. Spoon the batter into the slow cooker's pot insert and spread until evenly distributed.

In another bowl, whisk together the ½ cup granulated sugar, the ⅔ cup cocoa powder, the light brown sugar, and coffee until dissolved. Pour the coffee mixture over the cake batter. Do not stir.

Select slow-cook low and cook for 3 hours. The cake will slightly pull away from the sides of the pot but will not be completely set. Turn off the slow cooker. If the cake seems too loose, turn off the slow cooker and let the cake sit for 10 to 20 minutes before serving. It should be served warm.

Going Bananas

If your bananas are underripe, put them on a sheet pan and pop them into a heated 250°F oven for 15 to 20 minutes until the peels blacken. The heat activates the bananas' sugars to speed up the ripening process. When cool enough to handle, remove the soft fruit from the peels. For over-ripe bananas, put them in the freezer—peel and all—until you need them. Perfect for baking or smoothies.

Banana S'Mores Pie

In this recipe, s'mores, those campfire favorites of roasted marshmallows, chocolate squares, and graham crackers, meet banana cream pie, another American classic. With a store-bought pie crust, chocolate chips, Marshmallow Fluff, bananas, and whipped topping, this pie is an express-lane winner.

MAKES 8 SERVINGS

1 cup plus 3 tablespoons mini semisweet chocolate chips

⅔ cup heavy cream

1 9-inch graham cracker pie crust

1 7-ounce jar Marshmallow Fluff

1 8-ounce container nondairy whipped topping, chilled

2 ripe bananas

Put the 1 cup mini chocolate chips in a bowl. Set aside.

Heat the cream in a saucepan over medium-low heat until hot. Do not boil. Pour the hot cream over the chocolate chips to make a ganache. Let the ganache sit for a minute, then stir until smooth. Pour the ganache into the pie crust. Refrigerate until the chocolate is set, 20 to 25 minutes.

Put the marshmallow fluff and whipped topping in the bowl of an electric mixer. Beat on medium-high speed until light and fluffy, about 2 minutes.

To assemble the pie, slice the bananas into ¼-inch rounds and place them on top of the ganache. Spread the marshmallow topping over the bananas Sprinkle the 3 tablespoons mini chocolate chips on top. Refrigerate the pie for 4 hours or overnight before serving.

 SUPERMARKETSHORTCUTS

graham cracker pie crust • Marshmallow Fluff • nondairy whipped topping

Chocolate Chip Cookie Pie

When I was working in TV news in Altoona, Pennsylvania, I was happy to accept dinner invitations because I made so little money that I was usually broke. The hostess who served this dessert cautioned me to take a smaller than usual slice of this pie because it is so rich. She wasn't kidding. This is the most decadent pie you'll ever taste. While the pie is baking, your house will smell like Willie Wonka's chocolate factory.

MAKES 8 TO 10 SERVINGS

2 large eggs
½ cup granulated sugar
½ cup (packed) light brown sugar
1 teaspoon pure vanilla extract
¼ teaspoon table salt
¾ cup (1½ sticks) unsalted butter, softened and cut into 1-inch pieces
¾ cup all-purpose flour
1 cup semisweet chocolate chips
1 9-inch unbaked deep-dish pie crust

Heat the oven to 325°F. Place an oven rack in the lower third of the oven. Line a sheet pan with aluminum foil.

Whisk together the eggs, granulated and brown sugars, vanilla, and salt in the bowl of an electric mixer on high speed until the mixture is thick, pale yellow, and doubled in size, 4 to 5 minutes. Add the butter and beat on medium-high speed until combined. There will be tiny pieces of butter the size of panko bread crumbs in the batter. Lower the speed, add the flour, and mix on medium speed until incorporated. Using a rubber spatula, stir in the chocolate chips. Evenly spread the batter in the pie crust. Put the pie on the prepared sheet pan.

Bake until a knife inserted halfway between the edge and center comes out clean, 60 to 65 minutes. Remove from the oven and cool on a wire rack for 25 to 30 minutes. Cut into wedges to serve.

SUPERMARKETSHORTCUT

frozen pie crust

Key Lime Tartlets

If you're looking for a taste of summertime all year round, these individual tarts are perfect. Start with premade graham cracker tartlet shells. Using always available bottled Key lime juice means you don't have to spend time squeezing the small limes even if you can find them. Spoon on whipped topping and garnish with a slice of lime for a final finish.

MAKES 8 SERVINGS

8 individual graham cracker tartlet shells

1 14-ounce can sweetened condensed milk

3 large egg yolks

½ cup bottled Key lime juice

2 teaspoons grated lime zest

Nondairy whipped topping or canned whipped cream

2 thin slices lime, cut in quarters

Heat the oven to 350°F. Arrange the tartlet shells on a sheet pan.

Put the condensed milk and egg yolks into the bowl of an electric mixer and beat on low speed until incorporated. Add the lime juice and zest and mix until well combined. Evenly divide the filling mixture among the tartlet shells. Bake until the filling is set but still a little loose in the center, 10 to 12 minutes.

Let the tarts cool on a wire rack for 15 minutes. Once cooled, individually cover each with plastic wrap and refrigerate for at least 1 hour or overnight. Just before serving, place a dollop of whipped topping in the center of each pie and garnish with a piece of lime.

 SUPERMARKETSHORTCUTS

individual graham cracker tartlet shells • sweetened condensed milk • Key lime juice • nondairy whipped topping or canned whipped topping

Almond Biscotti Bread Pudding

Biscotti means "twice baked" in Italian. First, the cookie dough is shaped into a long log and baked. Then the log is sliced into individual pieces and baked again until they are crisp on all sides. Using store-bought biscotti is much less time consuming and makes this dessert a snap to put together.

MAKES 8 SERVINGS

Vegetable oil spray
3 cups whole milk
4 large eggs
⅔ cup sugar
½ teaspoon table salt
½ teaspoon almond extract

8 ounces Italian bread, cut into
 1½-inch cubes (8 cups)
8 almond biscotti, coarsely crushed
¼ cup slivered almonds
Confectioners' sugar

Heat the oven to 375°F. Coat a 9 x 13-inch baking dish with vegetable oil spray.

Whisk together the milk, eggs, sugar, salt, and almond extract in a bowl. Add the bread cubes and crushed biscotti and gently toss until most of the liquid is absorbed.

Pour the mixture into the prepared pan and distribute evenly. Sprinkle the almonds on top. Bake until golden brown and a knife inserted 2½ inches from the edge of the dish comes out clean, about 30 minutes. Let cool for 10 minutes before serving. Sift a dusting of confectioners' sugar over each portion.

 **SUPERMARKET**SHORTCUT

biscotti

Lemon Cooler Cookies

As a child I used to hoard my own box of these tart, crumbly, lemony cookies. Sadly, they were discontinued in 1996, but now you can make them at home.

MAKES 30 TO 34 COOKIES

1¾ cups all-purpose flour

1¾ teaspoons baking powder

¼ teaspoon table salt

½ cup (1 stick) unsalted butter, softened

⅔ cup plus ⅓ cup confectioners' sugar

⅓ cup granulated sugar

1 tablespoon grated lemon zest

1 large egg

1 teaspoon Kool-Aid Lemonade Unsweetened Drink Mix

Heat the oven to 350°F. Line two baking sheets with parchment paper.

Whisk together the flour, baking powder, and salt in a bowl. Put the butter in the bowl of an electric mixer and beat on high until smooth and creamy. Add the ⅔ cup confectioners' sugar, the granulated sugar, and lemon zest. Mix on medium speed until creamy. Add the egg and beat until combined. Reduce the speed to medium-low, add the flour mixture, and mix until a stiff dough forms.

Divide and shape the dough into 1-inch balls. Place the balls on the prepared baking sheets about 2 inches apart. Using the palm of your hand, flatten each to a thickness of ½ inch.

Bake until the cookies are firm to the touch but not browned, 12 to 14 minutes. Remove the cookies from the oven and let sit for a couple of minutes just until they are cool enough to touch.

Whisk the remaining ⅓ cup confectioners' sugar and the lemonade mix together in a bowl. Gently toss the cookies in the mixture until coated. Let cool on a wire rack for 30 minutes. Store in an airtight container at room temperature.

 SUPERMARKETSHORTCUT

Kool-Aid Lemonade Unsweetened Drink Mix

Peach Enchiladas

My mother has a dear group of girlfriends who call themselves "The Golden Girls." Mom told me about this dessert after one of the girls served it at their monthly card game. I put my own spin on these sweet enchiladas by adding cream cheese to the filling for richness. Serve them warm with a scoop of vanilla ice cream or whipped cream. I learned how to cook from the best, my mom. And I'm still learning.

MAKES 16, SERVES 8

2 8-ounce tubes refrigerated Pillsbury Original Crescent Rolls

1 8-ounce package cream cheese, cut into 16 cubes

1 15.25-ounce can sliced peaches, drained

⅔ cup (11 tablespoons) unsalted butter

1 cup sugar

1½ teaspoons ground cinnamon

1 12-ounce can lemon-lime-flavored soft drink, such as Sprite

Heat the oven to 350°F.

Take the crescent rolls out of the package. Separate the perforated triangles. Place 1 cream cheese cube and 1 peach slice on the wide end of a triangle. Roll up, starting at the wide end, then pinch the seams closed. Repeat with the remaining rolls, cream cheese, and peaches. Put the 16 peach enchiladas, pointed side down, in a 9 x 13-inch baking pan.

Melt the butter in a saucepan over medium-low heat. Remove the saucepan from the heat and stir in the sugar and cinnamon. Pour the butter mixture evenly over the rolls and then pour the soft drink all over as well.

Bake until golden brown and bubbly, about 45 minutes. Let rest for 15 minutes prior to serving.

 **SUPERMARKET**SHORTCUTS

Pillsbury Original Crescent Rolls • canned sliced peaches • lemon-lime soft drink

Easy Chocolate Truffles

With just four ingredients, these lush chocolate bites come together in no time. Store them on your countertop during cool weather or in the refrigerator when it's hot. I serve them at room temperature so they're creamy. For a bit of a twist, consider replacing half or all of the chocolate sprinkles with cocoa powder, grated coconut, or finely chopped nuts. It wouldn't hurt my feelings if you dipped them into softened creamy peanut butter, too.

MAKES 42 TO 46 TRUFFLES

1 14-ounce can sweetened condensed milk

3 tablespoons instant espresso coffee granules

12 ounces (60% cacao) bittersweet chocolate, broken up into small pieces

Chocolate sprinkles, for coating

Heat the milk and coffee granules in a saucepan over medium-low heat. Cook, whisking occasionally, until the mixture is hot but not boiling.

Remove the saucepan from the heat. Stir in the chocolate, whisking until it is completely melted. Pour the mixture into a bowl. Place a piece of plastic wrap directly on the surface of the mixture. Cover the bowl tightly with another piece of plastic wrap and refrigerate until cool, 1½ to 2 hours.

Pour the chocolate sprinkles into a small, shallow bowl. Using a tablespoon measure or a melon baller, shape the chocolate mixture into small balls. Roll each ball in the palms of your hands to gently warm it, and immediately toss it into the sprinkles to coat completely. Store in an airtight container.

 **SUPERMARKET**SHORTCUTS

sweetened condensed milk • instant espresso coffee granules

Black Forest Cake-Batter Milkshake

Licking the batter—especially chocolate—from the beaters was always a treat when my mom baked a cake. One of my favorite chocolate cakes is German Black Forest cake with dark chocolate layers, cherry filling, and whipped cream. To make this cake-in-a-glass milkshake, chocolate cake mix and canned cherries along with chocolate ice cream and cherry juice are whipped up in a blender. Each glass is topped with whipped cream, chocolate curls, and, of course, a cherry or two on top. This milkshake literally takes the cake.

MAKES 4 SERVINGS

2 cups chocolate ice cream
1 ½ cups cherry juice cocktail
½ cup canned pitted dark sweet
   cherries, drained, plus 8 for garnish

½ cup dry chocolate cake mix
Canned whipped cream
Chocolate curls

Put the ice cream, cherry juice, the ½ cup sweet cherries, and the cake mix into a blender. Blend until smooth, 30 to 35 seconds. Do not overblend or the milkshake will become too thin.

Divide the milkshake among four glasses and top each with a swirl of whipped cream. Garnish each one with chocolate curls and 2 cherries.

 SUPERMARKETSHORTCUTS

cherry juice cocktail • pitted cherries • chocolate cake mix • canned whipped cream • chocolate curls

Microwave Peanut Brittle

Wait until you taste this amazing peanut brittle! Since it's made in the microwave, there's no need to buy a special candy thermometer or worry about how long to cook the sugar. Substitute your favorite nuts (cashews, pecans, walnuts) and seeds (pumpkin and sunflower) or a combination. Nut brittle makes a delightful hostess or holiday gift as well—if you're willing to share it with anyone.

The recipe is based on using an 1100-watt microwave, which is what I have at home. If you have a 900- to 1000-watt microwave, adjust the recipe by increasing the cooking time after stirring in the butter, vanilla, and peanuts. Test in 10- to 15-second bursts.

MAKES 8 SERVINGS

1 cup sugar

⅓ cup light corn syrup

1 tablespoon unsalted butter

1¼ teaspoons pure vanilla extract

1¼ cups roasted peanuts

1 teaspoon baking soda

Line a sheet pan with a silicone mat or parchment paper.

Put the sugar and corn syrup in a microwave-safe bowl. Stir the sugar until it is completely moistened with the corn syrup. Microwave the mixture on high for 4 minutes.

Stir in the butter, vanilla, and peanuts until combined. Microwave on high for 3½ minutes.

Add the baking soda and stir for 1 minute, or until the mixture becomes foamy and turns light caramel in color.

Carefully pour the mixture onto the prepared pan. Using a rubber spatula, spread the mixture into a thin, even layer. Allow the brittle to cool completely, then break into pieces. Store in an airtight container at room temperature.

Cookies and Cream Dip

Here's the problem when I make this incredible dip: I keep sneaking to the fridge to steal another spoonful before company arrives. The classic American combination of crisp chocolate cookies and smooth cream is that good! Fold in the crumbled wafers just before serving so they don't become soggy. Arrange the strawberries, pound cake squares, and apple wedges on a platter to accompany the dip.

MAKES 3½ CUPS

1 8-ounce package cream cheese, at room temperature
2 tablespoons light brown sugar
2 teaspoons pure vanilla extract
¾ cup confectioners' sugar
2½ cups nondairy whipped topping
2 cups crushed Nabisco Famous Chocolate Wafers

Put the cream cheese, brown sugar, and vanilla into the bowl of an electric mixer. Beat on medium speed until creamy. Lower the speed, add the confectioners' sugar, and continue mixing until the mixture is smooth and fluffy. Add the whipped topping and mix on low until well incorporated.

If serving immediately, use a spatula to fold in the crushed wafers and serve.

To make ahead, cover and refrigerate the dip without the crushed wafers. About 1½ hours before serving, remove the dip from the refrigerator and fold in the crushed chocolate wafers.

 SUPERMARKETSHORTCUTS

nondairy whipped topping • Nabisco Famous Chocolate Wafers

Acknowledgments

Love and thanks to my family, especially my sweet mother, Sarah. All of my life you've taught me about balance in cooking and sharing joy around the table. You are my hero and my heart. I love you!

To my dear friends, your love and friendship are my great treasures. First, special thanks to Jimmy D'Angelo, Dewey, and Cosmo—the amazing trio. Also, Jane (Honey), Tara, Ed, Jill, Carolyn, Gail, Bob, Mikey, and Toni. We've eaten together, laughed together, and grown together. I am lucky to know all of you.

My *In the Kitchen with David* team: Liz Furlong, my friend, my rock, and my show partner. Stacey Stauffer, you bring beauty, laughter, and expertise to our show. I adore you. Additional thanks to Joe Kelly, Melissa Gulli, Lydia Thomas, Kate Matelan, Caitlyn McTear, Kelsey Brown, Leslie Soster, Madison Keefe, Morgan Hart, Kathleen Filachek, Jacqueline Culp, Brooke Moore, Judy Mosteller, Mike Saporetti, Sean Hagan, Justin Winters, Jamir Ricks, Chuck Puleo, Jess Sheppard, Megan Murphy, Christy Mitchell, Caroline Barbier, Maureen Siman, Melissa Kennedy, Alicia Rudd, Tara Cahill, Shannon Powlick, and Elizabeth Browde. Putting on this show takes a village and I'm honored to be a part of ours!

Special thanks to our QVC culinary styling team led by Adam Cavanaugh,

Bonne Ditomo, Jeri Estok, and Lynn Willis. Also, to all of our talented chef-stylists who make our show beautifully delicious.

Mary Ricks, you are amazing! You keep me on schedule, you keep my life organized, and you are my dear friend. I couldn't do any of this without you.

Cookbook Project Manager Susan Leibenhaut, you are an angel that dropped out of the sky and made this whole book come together. I can't thank you enough.

My dear Harriet Bell. This is our third book together and we now officially share a brain. I'm so grateful for your talent, but even more grateful for your friendship.

Pamela Cannon, my editor at Penguin Random House. You and the Ballantine team have been great partners. Thank you so much.

My photography team led by the amazing Tina Rupp. I felt at home with you from the first photo. Your photography makes each dish mouthwatering. Special thanks also to Johanna Halsmith-Weisser for your beautiful photos; you are an artist. To my buddy Wes Weisser for documenting this journey through your photos and videography.

My cookbook culinary leader, Stephen Delaney, and culinary team member, Andrea Schwob. You both made each recipe so wonderful and delicious. Thanks for your mad kitchen skills and the countless trips to the grocery store!

My creative director and team leader, Louise Bolin. Thank you for your amazing expertise, eye for detail, and your hugs. I have a new friend for life. Thanks also to assistant designer Rachael Deeringer, creative support Gabrielle Gorney, and creative support Antonia Olszowka.

My project and production team: Sherry Soldon, Carol Cotton, Dan Porto, Laura Chiquoine, and Pat Sanborn. You all came together and made the book's concepts happen so beautifully.

To our QVC management team: Steve Hofmann, you absolutely made this book possible. Thank you for your tremendous support. John Wall, you made the creative team happen and I'm so grateful. Thanks to Jack Comstock for your support, advice, and encouragement. Tim Bertoni for helping work out logistics and finding kitchen space to test recipes.

To Christina Pennypacker and Mamey Roope, my QVC cookbook buyers. You both are such incredible partners. Thanks for your vision, expertise, and all of your hard work.

Thanks to my image team: Tara Stewart for working tirelessly on my wardrobe. Karen Zaffarano, my makeup stylist. Thank you for making me look presentable and always powdered. You are a friend and an artist.

To Valerie Bertinelli for your friendship and wonderful energy. You are so kind to have written my foreword. It's so cool to think that I grew up watching you and I can now call you a friend. Big hug!

Finally, to my Foodies who watch *In the Kitchen with David* every Sunday and Wednesday. I am so grateful to each one of you! Our show has become one big family and I cherish the time we spend together. You inspire me each day to reach further and work harder, so we can all enjoy great food together. I humbly thank you.

Index

Page numbers of photographs appear in italics.

About the Author

DAVID VENABLE, bestselling cookbook author and accomplished home cook, is QVC's Resident Foodie, program-hosting on the network since 1993 with more than ten thousand hours of live television under his belt. He debuts two new recipes each week on his hit show *In the Kitchen with David*. Since the launch of the first series companion cookbook, followed by *Back Around the Table*, Venable has appeared on *Today*, *The Chew*, and *The Rachael Ray Show*, among others. His recipes have appeared in *People*, *HuffPost*, and many other publications. Venable has received praise from the food world for his easy, comforting cooking style, and he regularly connects with his foodies on QVC.com as well as Facebook, Twitter, and Instagram. Prior to joining QVC, Venable earned his bachelor's degree from the University of North Carolina, Chapel Hill, then worked as a television news anchor/reporter in West Virginia and Pennsylvania.

Facebook.com/DavidVenableQVC
Twitter: @DavidVenableQVC
Instagram: @davidvenableqvc